HOW TO STOP OVERTHINKING

A Step-by-Step Guide to Stop Overthinking, Stop Negative Thoughts, Declutter Your Mind, and Start Thinking Positively.

By

Thomas Jackson

© *2020 Thomas Jackson*

All rights reserved.

The following book, which is replicated here, was written with the objective of presenting information that is as accurate and trustworthy as possible. Even if you don't agree with the content of the book, purchasing it can be interpreted as your acknowledgment that neither the publisher nor the author of this book are experts on the topics covered in it, and that any recommendations or suggestions made in it are strictly for entertainment purposes only. Professionals should be contacted as required prior to executing any of the actions recommended in this document.

If this declaration isn't fair or legitimate, it can be legally enforced in all of the United States of America. The American Bar Association didn't think it was fair or legitimate.

Moreover, whether done electronically or in print, the transmission, replication, or reproduction of any of the following works, including any particular information included within, will be regarded as unlawful conduct. This includes making a secondary or tertiary copy of the work, as well as making a recorded recording of the work, and it is only permitted with the explicit written authorization of the publisher. There are no extra rights for this work.

It is generally agreed that the information contained in the following pages is a truthful and accurate representation of the facts, and as such, any reader who fails to pay attention to, or who uses or misuses, the information in question will be solely responsible for any actions that result from their failure to do so. There are no situations in which the publisher or the original author of this book may be held accountable in any way for any difficulty or damage that may befall them as a result of following the instructions included in this document.

Furthermore, the material included on the following pages is meant solely for informative purposes and should not be construed as being universal in nature. In keeping with its nature, it is supplied with no warranty as to the long-term validity or interim quality of the information. They don't get permission from the trademark owner to use their names. This should not be seen as an endorsement from the trademark owner, though.

Table of contents

INTRODUCTION 5

STEP ONE: IDENTIFY YOUR ENEMY AND THE CAUSES OF YOUR OVERTHINKING. 8

STOP OVERTHINKING THINGS. 16

STEP TWO: 10 POWERFUL ACTIONS TO ELIMINATE ANXIETY AND WORRYING RESULTS FOREVER 29

STEP THREE: REFRESHING YOUR MIND FROM A NEGATIVE ATTITUDE 59

STEP FOUR: IN JUST A FEW MINUTES, YOU CAN LEARN HOW TO STOP OVERTHINKING AND GET RID OF NEGATIVE THOUGHTS BY FOLLOWING THE STEPS IN THIS ARTICLE. 75

STEP FIVE: USING POSITIVITY 98

STEP SIX: LEARN HOW TO DECLUTTER YOUR MIND AND BECOME THE PERSON YOU WANT TO BE IN LIFE. 115

STEP SEVEN: IMPLEMENT SIMPLE DAILY PRACTICES TO GET RID OF PROCRASTINATION 154

CONCLUSION 180

INTRODUCTION

This book presents and explores methods for dealing with a hyperactive mind. The mental chatter or noise produced by your brain at night, in the morning, and during the day may make it difficult to live a tranquil existence. Most individuals get melancholy or anxious as a result of negative thinking, overthinking, and excessive worrying. This book discusses why you were diagnosed with a "disease" that you never requested, as well as how to manage and live with it. There are several ways that describe the various parts of mental chatter and how to conquer them gradually.

Do you find yourself lying awake at night because you can't stop thinking about what occurred the day before? Do you find yourself second-guessing almost every choice you make in your life? Is your work or your friendships becoming too much for you? Reading this book will give you the confidence to face your worries, cope with your perfectionism, and conquer your identified illnesses. Onc thing you may learn from this book is that your ideas do not determine your actions. You can expect to be aware of where your mental chatter originates from and how to manage it as you practice the methods and tactics in this book.

Stop thinking about what you accomplished today and begin living in the present now. Stop looking forward to tomorrow and start breathing in the joy of now. Stop overthinking your future and make significant adjustments to experience it now. We are only given today, so instead of stressing about what you might have done at that social function or attempting to control what you will do at your next appointment, learn to breathe in the present now.

Perhaps the most important thing you can take away from reading this book is that your ideas decide the fate of your life. Even though this is a tough statement to accept (particularly for those of you who are more on your mind than ever before), all you need to do right now is learn positivism. This book will go through the reasons why the way you think right now isn't good for you, as well as how optimism may substantially improve and achieve the results you desire in your life. So, stop being trapped, stop allowing your thoughts to dominate you, and take charge of what you desire. Finally, there are lessons and a framework to help you get to where you want to go, rather than where you are now. And it's all written down in this book.

STEP ONE: IDENTIFY YOUR ENEMY AND THE CAUSES OF YOUR OVERTHINKING.

Overthinking occurs when you are unable to get anything off your mind and have uncontrolled or intrusive thoughts that do not seem to go away. It occurs when you overanalyze everything around you or are unable to think properly owing to an excessive number of ideas overwhelming your head. In practically every circumstance, overthinking implies dwelling on what might have been, what should have occurred, or the "what ifs."

When you overthink, your mind traps you in vicious thought-cycles or thinking patterns. It's as if you're mentally fatigued all the time because your brain can't relax or shut down. It is easy to get caught up in your own head since the world and universe we live in compel us to think about everything we do, wish, and believe. Stress, anxiety, sadness, and other mood disorders are caused by overthinking. Over thinkers are always concerned with their obligations, whether they are decent people, if they are making the correct decisions, and whether they are productive or unproductive. Because ideas lead to actions, and actions lead to character, thoughts shape who we are or wish to be as people. With so much to think about on a daily basis, it's no surprise that our minds are working overtime.

Do you know whether you overthink things? Maybe you believe you do, but then you second-guess yourself and persuade yourself that you don't, prompting you to re-ask your initial question. Do I overanalyze everything? Overthinking is a way of life for certain individuals, and they can't help but worry about everything. It is difficult to manage or even halt overthinking once it has begun.

Here are some indications that your mind has you locked and is in overdrive:

1. Sleeplessness

Insomnia occurs when individuals are unable to turn off their thoughts. You may be fatigued during the day, yet when you lie down to sleep or relax, you are suddenly awake. Your mind is filled with everything you haven't done yet, everything you want to accomplish, or maybe you didn't perfect what you previously did. Your mind obsesses over matters over which you have no control or over which you could have controlled but did not. This is when you find yourself imprisoned in a mental institution. This is also known as overthinking, and it leads to the development of sleeplessness.

2. BEING ANXIOUS

If you can't rest until you've considered and prepared for every possible possibility for what's to come or what hasn't occurred yet, it's an indication that you're locked within your own thoughts. Most individuals who are unable to stop overthinking resort to drugs, alcohol, or prescription medicine to drown out their thoughts in order to find calm. If your thoughts are making you uncomfortable, and you are afraid of the unknown and seem to require control, this is a symptom that you are living in fear and have been caught in your mind.

3. OVERTHINKING EVERYTHING IN YOUR SURROUNDINGS

Much like the preceding symptom, the drive to control is overpowering and is one of the primary concerns associated with overthinking behaviors. The urge to control everything implies that you attempt to prepare for the unknown future, so you dread failure and stress over what you are doing now to prevent negative things from occurring. You are not living in the present moment, which causes you great tension since your mind is preoccupied with everything else. Someone who over-analyzes things has a difficult time embracing change, since change is seldom planned, which puts them into a downward spiral because they are suddenly confronted with something over which they have no control. Overthinking leads to poor decision-making abilities as a result of indecision on what to do next.

4. Anxiety about failure (also known as perfectionism)

Perfectionists like controlling things as well. However, they manage projects and their surroundings, ensuring that everything is done correctly in order to avoid making a mistake. Perfectionists are incapable of accepting failure and will go to tremendous measures to prevent it. As a consequence of this tendency, perfectionists would avoid making large choices or embracing significant chances because they would prefer to do nothing than take the risk of failing.

5. DOUBTFUL SELF-EVALUATION

Because of the overpowering fear of failure and perfectionism, the mind of a "control freak" would often analyze, reanalyze, second-guess, and come up with another analysis, until nothing seemed good enough, and the circle continues. Someone who is unable to embrace change or who does not completely trust in themselves may second-guess themselves out of fear of making the incorrect action or choice. They also take twice as long to comprehend information because they second-guess others and wonder whether they understood the dialogue correctly. Consider yourself an over-thinker if this occurs to you.

6. MIGRAINES

Headaches occur as a consequence of second-guessing and overthinking things, since the mind cannot manage to find any calm for even a minute. Headaches are an indication that we need to relax or unwind. It is an indication that we need to cope or find ways to calm our brains and bodies. Body tightness, which is an indication of stress, may also cause headaches.

7. MUSCLE ACHES AND STIFFNESS IN THE JOINTS

One of the leading causes of stress is overthinking. When you continue to overthink, your brain associates it with how things should be and, as a consequence, traps you. This results in negative and overpowering thinking patterns, compulsive worrying, anxiety, OCD, and other mood or stress-related problems. When a person is extremely anxious or overthinks, it affects their whole body. Only when you identify and address the source of your stress or troubles will the pain and pains go away. When your brain attacks your muscles and body, your emotions and mood are impacted as well, leaving you lethargic and emotionally drained or fatigued.

8. TIREDNESS

As mentioned in the previous symptom, we will feel exhausted if we take on more than our bodies and thoughts can bear. Fatigue is your body's warning sign that you are going to exhaust yourself. Burnouts are unavoidable if you are always on the go, not only physically but also emotionally. It's similar to an electrical gadget that requires batteries; if it's kept on 24/7 or continues to play without being charged, it will die or need battery replacement. Fatigue is the brain's way of telling you that it needs to recharge or that you need to relax since you are running out of energy.

9. IT IS NOT PERMITTED TO BE PRESENT.

Do you find yourself attempting to listen to what people are saying but being distracted by your own thoughts? Or, do you find yourself attempting to be present with your children or spouse, but are too preoccupied with what you need, what has to be done, or what has been overlooked (since there has to be something)? This indicates your mind has ensnared you in the delightful realm of overthinking. Isn't it fantastic? Not... Too much thinking might lead you to lose concentration or lose sight of what is most essential in life. Slow down, since not everything has to be hurried. After all, you still have a life to live and a life to lead.

As you can see, these symptoms, or indicators of overthinking, are related to one another. For example, you may begin overanalyzing and second-guessing things as a result of your fear of failure, which causes anxiety as a result of your lack of control over the uncertain future. When this occurs, headaches and tight muscles develop, which leads to a lack of sleep, resulting in insomnia and weariness, complicating matters and making it difficult to remain in the present moment. Overthinking and excessive worrying are difficult to manage, but there is some hope.

By the conclusion of this book, you will have developed an understanding of precisely what to change and how to do it without fear of the repercussions. Consider this book to be your thorough guide to getting healthier and leaving those troublesome ideas in the dust as you read on.

STOP OVERTHINKING THINGS.

Wouldn't you leap at the chance to halt your thoughts if there was such a thing or ability? Consider being able to obtain more rest and calm your thoughts in order to discover tranquility. This is achievable, but patience, determination, motivation, and resilience must be developed. In the next chapters, I will go over additional ways to stop overthinking and worrying for good, but for now, let's concentrate on how to stop overthinking.

You must be patient since not everyone becomes an expert at relaxing their mind overnight. Resilience is required because you must be conscious that you may fail, but practice makes perfect. Every day that you practice mind-quieting brings you one step closer to the benefits of inner peace and living consciously. Also, we'll go over why it's so crucial to stay motivated and address your overthinking behaviors later on.

Overthinking is perfectly natural once in a while, but when it develops into a habit that ultimately spreads and continues to impair your daily life, it has become a problem. There are two mental processes that include negative overthinking:

- **Ruminating-Reminiscing about the past**

Overthinking things you can't alter or worrying over things that have happened are examples of ruminating thoughts. For example, suppose you attended a meeting and expressed your viewpoint on a certain issue; subsequently, you tell yourself you shouldn't have done so, and you worry over what you might have said better. Furthermore, negative thinking originates from ruminating on ideas, such as thinking about something someone said about you that was unfavorable and then believing it because of something you did previous to this thought. For example, you recall classmates or peers telling you that you wouldn't go far, and you're beginning to believe them.

- **·Excessive concern-Making pessimistic predictions about the future**

You might sit there and convince yourself that you're not going to be able to deliver a nice presentation tomorrow. Alternatively, you might sit there and believe that you aren't good enough, which causes your spouse or partner to find someone else. You don't trust yourself, so you're not confident in how things will turn out since you're afraid of the unknown future.

Over thinkers create worst-case scenarios and get worried as a result of these "visions." It's one thing to think badly and fret or obsess over terrible outcomes or experiences; it's quite another to have visuals or photographic images play in your head. Assume you're going to pick up your kids from school, and you have five minutes until they're outside waiting for you. Your vehicle breaks down on the route to their school, forcing you to call for assistance. Your mind sends you a picture or "vision" of your children waiting, no one present to pick them up, and suddenly a stranger arrives to take them up, and your children are gone. You begin to feel uneasy, and your mind plays tricks on you, convincing you that you are a lousy parent or carer. This is the mental trap that overthinking creates. When this occurs, take a minute to consider and not only call for assistance, but also phone the school and inform the principal of what has occurred before making another call for someone else to pick up your children. When you take a minute to pause and consider the best-case scenario, your mind doesn't have time to worry about what is unreasonable and unlikely to occur.

According to one study[1], overthinking cause's mental health problems and decreased sleep, which leads to the use of alcohol or drugs as a coping mechanism? So, let's get started on figuring out how to terminate this ruminating, over-worrying nightmare. Use the following ways to get some peace and quiet up there, as well as more restful nights:

1. RECOGNIZE WHEN YOU'RE OVERTHINKING.

Develop your self-awareness. When you do this, you will be more aware of when those troublesome ideas arise. The first step to breaking the cycle is to be aware of your triggers and what the first indicator of being locked in the overthinking habit is. When you discover yourself worrying over things you can't control or fretting about the past, recognize them and note their presence without becoming nervous or judge mental. Tell yourself that you will take 10 minutes to think about whatever is bothering you. Make a timer. Recognize that thinking this way isn't useful since it won't alter anything, and then go on to whatever else is bothering you. After you've finished this procedure, take several deep breaths and do anything else to divert your attention.

2. EXAMINE YOUR ASSUMPTIONS.

Challenging your ideas is a beneficial technique to break out of the negative, overthinking loop that your mind wants you to remain in. If you find yourself believing that you will be fired or that you will be evicted from your house because you are late, take a step back.

Consider the best-case scenario if you find yourself fretting about things that hasn't occurred yet. If you can't help but think about the worst-case situation, consider ways to avoid having the worst-case scenario occur. For example, if your alarm didn't go off and you're going to be late to work, instead of listening to your ideas and rushing about, confront your thoughts. Consider what you can accomplish. Can you phone in and let them know you're going to be late? Will you be able to arrive on time? What can you do to make sure this doesn't happen again? Is it worth it to fret about being perfect? Recognize and accept that no one is flawless. When you take a step back and think about things rationally, you'll notice that things go quicker and easier.

3. FOCUS ON PROBLEM-SOLVING.

Work on problem-solving strategies in the same manner that you would challenge your thinking. Why ruminate on issues when you can fix them? Rather than pondering why something happened, consider what you can do about it. When you take action and consider solutions to issues and stresses, you educate your brain that you are in charge, and it rewires itself to automatically handle problems successfully the more you practice. So, instead of tearing yourself apart, take additional time to calm down and address the situation. Look for answers and consider how you might make a difference. If it cannot be altered, let it go and concentrate on something else.

4. Put Mindfulness into Practice and Investigate It.

Mindfulness is a fantastic skill that may benefit everyone in the present moment. Being aware means being present in the moment. It implies that nothing else matters save this moment, place, and existence. It is to be at one with oneself and one's ideas. Consider this: how can you concentrate on the past or the future if you are consciously paying attention to the here and now? With practice, mindfulness is an excellent strategy for minimizing overthinking and negative thoughts.

5. Change the Channel.

What would you do if I told you not to think about a purple elephant bouncing on pink clouds? You will, no matter how hard you try, think about the elephant's color and what it is doing. The same is true while attempting to cease doing something. As a result, telling oneself not to think about something is sure to backfire. Instead, recognize your thoughts and do something different to divert yourself, such as exercise or calling a buddy to vent and listening to them rant. When you concentrate on other people or things, you are more inclined to do something other than overthinking and worrying. Another fruitful option is to be innovative. Create a visual representation of your ideas, compose a diary entry, or rhyme your current mood with other words. Play a scrabble game or interact with household items. Sometimes all it takes is getting out of the home, going outdoors, or moving away from where you are. This is also a method for "rebooting" your hyperactive mind. We'll go through this more later.

Finally, the more you use these tactics, the better you will get at quieting your thoughts. You will be able to think more clearly when your mind is at peace.

When you can think things through, you can make efficient judgments without being distracted by negative ideas. Over time, your mind will learn to filter out unneeded anxieties on its own, and you will feel less worried and be able to deal with difficulties more effectively.

How Deep Is Your Overthinking?

Now that we've covered the symptoms of overthinking and what you can do to prevent or reduce it, we'll look at how much of an over thinker you are. Overthinking may be caused by an underlying issue such as generalized anxiety disorder (GAD). GAD is characterized by uncontrolled worrying, anxiety, and tension buildup. The term "generalized anxiety disorder" refers to the fact that you don't dread just one thing, but virtually everything, since everything makes you worried owing to your obsessive thought-patterns. It only becomes a disorder when you are unable to control it and it begins to take over your life by causing situational symptoms or when you have "panic attacks" about your thoughts. The purpose of this part is to determine how much of an over thinker you are and if it is related to anxiety or another mood illness. This is a test you may complete online to see whether you have anxiety and what kind it is:

http://www.heretohelp.bc.ca/screening/online/?screen=anxiety

This is a test to see whether you are an over-thinker and, if so, how deep you are. It also includes helpful hints and information for understanding what it means to be an over thinker:

https://www.happierhuman.com/overthinking/

This is an online test to assess whether sadness is causing your overthinking patterns.

https://www.psycom.net/depression-test/

These tests are not intended to diagnose you, but rather to determine if you should see a doctor.

Is Overthinking a Mental Illness?

Based on your habits and life choices, you should already know whether you are an overthinker. So, the next thing is to determine if there is an underlying issue. Anxiety or sadness may be caused mostly by overthinking. This is because while we are locked in our heads, we are always worrying about things we believe we can control but cannot. When we continue to think badly and are unable to manage our thought-patterns that revolve around these negative ideas, we become sad. The answer to the question of whether overthinking is a disorder is yes. Many individuals also suffer from overthinking things, such as whether they made the proper decision or are on the "right" route.

The truth is that nothing is ever "right" or "wrong," but it is if we establish these notions inside our own brains and then attempt to achieve the objectives of what is right or bad. For example, when we first meet someone's family, we may wonder, "Did I say the proper thing?" Alternatively, "Did I create the "correct" impression?" In reality, this person's family isn't even considering or judging you based on your own views. As a result, nothing is "correct" or "wrong" in this sense.

When confronted with this "right or wrong" attitude or thinking, attempt to consciously concentrate on the present moment and practice mindfulness.

Overthinking only becomes a problem when it becomes your sole activity and interferes with your everyday necessities. Overthinking becomes a condition when you are unable to complete tasks or are afraid of making errors, resulting in anxiety, sadness, and other mood disorders. However, if you are just concerned about the same issues every day but do not allow them to influence your actions, you may not necessarily have an overthinking illness. If you are always concerned about yourself, your life, your health, your family, your friends, and so on, this may not be an indication of an overthinking illness. If you find yourself worried or being too concerned about other people's lives and their problems or anxieties, this may indicate that you have an empathic nature. So, how can you know whether you suffer from an overthinking disorder? One or more of the following symptoms indicate that you may be a sufferer:

- Because you have unrealistic expectations of yourself, you compare yourself to others and question their assessments. You are continually concerned with what others think of you rather than being comfortable in your own skin.

- Spending too much time analyzing every possible event or incident in your life Thinking or envisioning the worst-case scenario leads to the belief that everything and everyone is "trying to get you."
- Inability to recover from setbacks or mistakes. Constantly ruminating on how you could have done things differently, or what you should or should not have said or done, and then experiencing extreme uneasiness and anxiety as a result.
- Setting "impossible" goals and believing you will never be able to achieve them. Establish objectives that you can realistically achieve, so you feel overwhelmed and don't do anything to strive towards them.
- The inability to switch off your hyperactive thoughts, which causes you to be tired and anxious all of the time.

If any of these symptoms appear or seem familiar to you, it is suggested that you get professional help for your mental health and to deal with your concerns and anxieties. You may benefit from the guidance of a professional, such as a doctor or therapist, who can teach you coping methods and other skills to help you manage overthinking and other mental illnesses. Because of your obsessive and perfectionist tendencies, you may also experience communication difficulties as a result of your inability to truly listen; you may find it difficult to enjoy hobbies or interests; and you may be unproductive at work as a result of your obsessive and perfectionist tendencies.

Other mood disorders, such as anxiety, generalized anxiety disorder (GAD), depression, insomnia, and obsessive-compulsive disorder (OCD), may become more apparent in your everyday life if you overthink things or are unable to "unwind."

Overthinking has now been defined, as well as the consequences it may have. As you go through this book, you will learn about more signs and causes of overthinking that we will cover in greater detail. In the next chapter, we will go through the symptoms of GAD, melancholy, and OCD in more detail since these mood disorders are generally defined by excessive worrying as their primary feature. If you've already been diagnosed or believe you're on the brink of being diagnosed, we'll go through the steps that you can take to get the care that you need. Specifically, I will explore worrying and tackling your fears in the next chapter. I will also go into further detail on what happens in the brain when you overthink or worry excessively.

Step Two: 10 Powerful Actions to Eliminate Anxiety and Worrying Results Forever

An excessive amount of worrying is another animal altogether. Tormenting oneself with thoughts of the past, present, and future is a sign of over-worrying, which is akin to overthinking. It's a state of mind in which you're continuously on edge, worried about the smallest of details. OCD, anxiety, and depression may all be caused by an individual's habit of over-worrying. Because we're afraid of facing our anxieties, it's tough to find a way to conquer them. As a result, we end up suffering. Over thinkers and extreme worry-warts may be distinguished from one another. Overthinking is a kind of denial, while worrying is a form of fear.

Fear: When we are worried, we are filled with self-doubt and a continual dread of the unknown, which makes it difficult to accept and deal with changes in our lives. The emotion of fear causes us to avoid doing things we really want to do because it traps us in our imaginations as a means of keeping us safe. Fear, on the other hand, is a deluding delusion. When we are afraid of change or the unknown, we lose out on possibilities that are right in front of us, such as a promotion, the opportunity to meet new people, and the opportunity to gain information that will help us improve ourselves. We'll speak more about fear and how to deal with it in a later lesson.

Denial: Most of the time, we deny what we desire, so we adhere to denial in order to avoid feeling uncomfortable or experiencing terrible feelings. We may use diversions such as drugs, alcohol, prescription medications, exercise, or work in order to deal with denial or to tolerate further denial from others. Distractions such as these might help us avoid facing our reality. Those who utilize ideas, on the other hand, are those who cannot or do not want to accept what is or what has happened. This causes overthinking in these people.

If you are unable to get control of your thoughts, which causes you to worry excessively, you will experience increased stress, which is also a primary cause of mental health issues. Fortunately, this book will provide you with insight into how to stop worrying in order to reduce the likelihood of disorders emerging and thus live a better life overall.

PROBLEMS WITH ONE'S MENTAL HEALTH

We provided a brief explanation of GAD in the previous chapter; therefore, we will go into greater detail about it today. The most succinct way to describe generalized anxiety disorder is that it is a condition in which concerns and anxieties take over your life and interfere with good routines, making it difficult to create healthy and productive behaviors. It's possible to be anxious about something in a useful manner, for example, by having an idea and recognizing it, thinking about it, and then letting it go. Why is this impact more beneficial? Because worrying does not take over your thoughts and you are still able to accomplish things you like doing since there is no overpowering anxiety about something you cannot control. It is easy to recognize that worrying will not change anything, and it is simple to divert yourself or think about other things. However, GAD has a completely different impact on the individual. People suffering with GAD find it very difficult to divert their attention away from their anxieties and intrusive thoughts. They anticipate the worst in every circumstance and experience the symptoms of an "anxiety attack" as a consequence of their brain and body being overworked and overstimulated. Patients suffering with generalized anxiety disorder (GAD) find it incredibly difficult to slow down and be in the present moment. Here are some indicators that someone may be suffering from generalized anxiety disorder.

EMOTIONAL

- Excessive worry and intrusive thoughts that is difficult to control or calm;
- No matter what they do, no one can get rid of intrusive or unpleasant thoughts that they have on a regular basis. Is unable to cope with uncertainty or change. They require information about, planning for, and control over their future.
- A feeling of dread or anxiety that appears unexpectedly as anxieties take control.

BEHAVIORAL

- They can't relax, are always tense, can't enjoy alone time, and don't seem to be able to decompress;
- They have difficulty concentrating or paying attention to tasks, jobs, or school;

- They regularly postpone or cancel activities or "to-dos" because they are overwhelmed by their anxieties.
- When they experience anxiety attacks in specific settings, they avoid going out or entering situations for fear of being overwhelmed by their thoughts and becoming overwhelmed themselves. They may also overthink the situation before the event, causing them to avoid going to or doing anything that may cause them worry.

PHYSICAL

- Constant muscle pressure or joint stiffness Throughout the day, the body feels strained;
- As a result of an overactive mind, restless nights become more prevalent and may progress to insomnia.
- Constantly feeling on edge or restless, with the ability to frighten easily;

Gastritis, nausea, diarrhea, and constipation are all symptoms of a gastrointestinal disorder.

This list of symptoms may seem overwhelming, but the good news is that with the correct advice and support, you can and will discover methods to deal with it all. Another illness that may develop as a result of excessive worrying is obsessive-compulsive disorder (OCD).

In contrast to anxiety disorders, OCD is defined by the need to take actions based on what you are thinking rather than being terrified of your thoughts and anxieties. As an example, someone suffering from OCD could find it necessary to wash their hands twenty times a day or count the number of red items in a room before they can do anything else. It does not provide joy to the person, but it does provide them with a means of dealing with their own worries. In OCD, unwelcome intrusive thoughts cause you to believe that you must perform repeated actions or engage in ritualized activities, such as counting or singing while bathing or tapping your fingers on a table. OCD may also cause you to move or arrange items in a certain manner. Because they cannot resist the need to do that precise thing, if these chores or behaviors are not accomplished exactly when the person believes they are required to complete them, it generates a great deal of anxiety.

For the uninitiated, it occurs when the brain becomes hooked on a certain concept or impulse that will not go away until it is exercised or repeated. It is similar to a CD or disk that skips when it is scratched, leaving the listener unable to finish the music. When this happens, the individual feels as though they are unable to continue their day unless they act on this notion or impulse that they have. Some indicators that you may be suffering from OCD are listed below:

THOUGHT

Germ phobia, which includes the fear of becoming contaminated as well as the fear of polluting others;

- Fear that you will lose control of yourself or your surroundings, causing you to injure yourself or others.
- unwanted and uncontrollable disturbing thoughts involving sexual or violent imagery;
- an overemphasis on religious or moral principles;
- Concerned about forgetting something or leaving something behind that you might require later.
- Adherence to superstitions;
- The idea or belief that everything has a place and that everything must be done in a specific or exact manner.

BEHAVIORS

- Re-inspection of appliances, lock mechanisms, clocks, and switches on a regular basis

- having excessive control over the safety of a loved one, to the point where you constantly check in on them
- Engaging in illogical behavior such as counting, tapping, repeating words or phrases, or relieving anxiety in a variety of ways.
- Keeping yourself or your surroundings clean on a regular basis;
- Arranging things exactly as you NEED them to be in order to avoid instilling fear and terror in others.
- Collecting "trash," which may include newspapers, pebbles, food containers, clothing, and other items.

Despite the fact that living with OCD or seeing someone else suffer with it may be distressing, treatment is available. Later on, we'll talk about how to stop or manage excessive worrying, and these tactics and advice will be useful for those who suffer from illnesses such as anxiety, depression, and OCD, among other things. When it comes to depression, this is another condition that may result from excessive anxiety.

There are two types of sorrow: sadness and depression. Depression is more than simply being in a gloomy or depressed mood; it is when our negative thoughts get uncontrolled and we see the world as nothing but a sea of gloom and gloominess. As this style of thinking becomes further entrenched in our minds, we lose interest in attempting or caring about anything, which causes us to become despondent and melancholy. Getting out of bed in the mornings might be tough, and you may find yourself losing interest in things that you would typically like. Depression interferes with your daily activities, interfering with vital behaviors such as eating, sleeping, working, and learning. People who suffer from depression describe it as a sensation of being empty or hopeless, which leads them to assume that there is no reason for life or that nothing can offer them pleasure. The following are the signs and symptoms of depression:

· A feeling of helplessness or emptiness. Overwhelming, black-and-white thinking, such as the belief that nothing will improve and that there is nothing you can or will do to change the situation; Inability to maintain an interest in previously enjoyed activities such as sex, hobbies, and socializing. You do not experience joy or pleasure, and you do not see a need for these emotions.

Changes in eating habits: you may lose weight as a result of a lack of interest in eating, or you may gain weight as a result of "eating your emotions."

Sleep disruptions are a problem. As a result of sleeplessness or the sense of pessimism that your brain creates about your life, you may find yourself sleeping excessively.

- Rage and rage-like feelings It seems like everything gets under your skin; your tolerance level is poor, you have a short fuse, and you have a short fuse.
- Tiredness or a sense of depletion Because of the persistent ideas that pass through your head on a daily basis, you feel weighed down and depleted of energy as a result of your routines, such as your sleeping and eating schedules.
- A lack of self-esteem You lack confidence and have a pessimistic outlook on yourself and other people's circumstances. Unwanted negative thoughts have worn you down to the point where you've given up hope and lost enthusiasm for improving your situation.
- Difficulties concentrating one's attention. As a result of your hyperactive mind, which continues to drag you down, you have a difficult time concentrating on chores, making judgments, and recalling information.

Because they both include comparable sensations and symptoms, it is easy to mistake depression for bipolar illness when they are not properly diagnosed. Bipolar disorder, on the other hand, is characterized by periods of high energy followed by periods of low depressive mood. People who suffer from this mental health condition have difficulty maintaining emotional balance or maintaining a stable "neutral" mood. Bipolar disease may be confused with other mental illnesses such as personality disorders or DE realization disorders.

As you can see, overthinking may lead to excessive worrying, which in turn can lead to negative thought patterns. This can have a significant impact on your mental health and well-being. If you believe you are experiencing any of the symptoms of any of the diseases listed above, it is important to seek medical attention or consult with a psychiatrist. On the other hand, try not to be too concerned or concerned about whether or not you experience these symptoms. The majority of people who read this book has not been diagnosed with a mental illness or has not experienced any of the symptoms described in this book. Continue reading to understand more about what happens in the brain, and then we'll get into the good practices that may help you reduce the ongoing tension that revolves around your anxious mind.

WHAT EXACTLY HAPPENS IN THE OVERACTIVE/WORRIED BRAIN IS A MYSTERY.

Now that we've learned more about the consequences of excessive worrying, let's look at how our brains function when we suffer from these conditions or spend our lives worrying on a regular basis. Did you know that the long-term consequences of stress may cause your brain to physically alter and seem different from one person to another? MRI (magnetic resonance imaging) scans of the brains of two individuals with diagnosed depression and two individuals who did not have diagnosed depression revealed that the brains of the individuals with diagnosed depression were somewhat different from the brains of the other two individuals. A magnetic resonance imaging (MRI) scan of the brain revealed that those suffering from persistent depression had a smaller hippocampus as well as a thinner right cortex. A portion of the brain called the hippocampus is responsible for memory, and a portion called the right cortex is responsible for our mood.

In light of the fact that depression is primarily characterized by the way we talk to ourselves and perceive the world, whether in a negative or positive light, it is reasonable to speculate that excessive worrying may be the root cause of the reduced activity of reward-processing regions in the brain. They are responsible for the "feel good" receptors such as serotonin and dopamine in the brain, which are controlled by the reward processors. The "feel good" hormones excite us about things such as hobbies, sociability, and new experiences, among other things. When this area of the brain is less active, it might be difficult to feel enthusiastic about these things.

When people are anxious for a long period of time, their serotonin and dopamine levels drop, resulting in increased degrees of sadness and anxiety in the affected individuals. If left untreated or unnoticed, it has the potential to worsen and create further difficulties. Take a look at what these compounds are capable of doing:

SEROTONIN:

Serotonin is a neurotransmitter that affects mood, emotions, and sleep. This molecule is responsible for helping you feel enthusiastic, for maintaining a good mood, and for making you feel less anxious or concerned overall. If you are continually worried, it is possible that your serotonin levels are lower than they should be.

DOPAMINE:

Dopamine is a neurotransmitter that influences subconscious action, cognitive awareness and attention, as well as pleasant emotions. Because significant quantities of dopamine are released into the bloodstream during sexual encounters and physical exertion, these activities may induce a euphoric sense in the participant. If your dopamine levels are low, you may find it difficult to focus or feel the desire to engage in activities that make you feel good about yourself.

NOREPINEPHRINE:

This molecule is responsible for the sensations of arousal, sleep, attention, and mood that we experience. Essentially, it combines the two other chemicals and stimulates the production of additional "feel good" receptors when we choose to engage in healthy behaviors or exercise self-control when we are nervous. Something that most people are unaware of concerning anxiety is that it is necessary for our body and spirit to be anxious in order to get us out of harmful circumstances, such as when we are engaged in a vehicle accident or fleeing away from something. Anxiety triggers the "fight, flight, or freeze" response, which is beneficial when we are faced with a life-threatening situation. These reactions are activated in our bodies, providing us with the adrenaline we need to carry out whatever action is required. When we are in a dangerous situation, chemicals and hormones in our bodies are activated, which sharpens our senses and helps us fight better, run faster, or remain quiet and silent for longer periods of time than we would otherwise. This is problematic because if we acquire an anxiety "disorder," our "fight, flight, or freeze" response is activated by erroneous concerns and may manifest itself either immediately or gradually. So, what is it in the brain that causes these "false alarm" triggers to be triggered in the first place? How many of you are aware of the fact that your brain is already developing ideas and habits and preparing to deliver physical symptoms before your body begins to experience the signs of an anxiety or panic attack?

For this reason, most psychologists or physicians would instruct you to pay attention to what you were thinking or doing just before the dread began to form inside of your body. Extraordinary fretting may precipitate an attack that develops as a result of mental patterns and everyday routines. The amygdala and hippocampus play a significant part in the majority of "worry warts," which manifest themselves as persistent anxiety or continual stress.

Amygdala:

In this portion of the brain, the connections between the parts of the brain that process incoming sensory information and the areas that comprehend these signals are established. It is a structure that resembles an almond and is found deep inside the cerebral cortex. This is the area of the brain that is responsible for triggering alarms or warnings of danger. In the amygdala, there is an emotional memory section, which may explain why some people are terrified by things such as sight (dogs, spiders, or flying) or smell (childhood smells or recognizable smells that signal danger), taste (food or other tastes that elicit paranoia or hypochondria, such as if someone has ever been poisoned), and sound (such as thunder) (noises, such as storms, banging cupboards, or yelling). Having said that, it is reasonable to suppose that post-traumatic stress disorder (PTSD) is caused by an overactive amygdala in certain people.

Hippocampus

Not only is the hippocampus a memory-related portion of the brain, but it is also responsible for transmitting potentially dangerous events. People who have experienced post-traumatic stress disorder (PTSD), child abuse, or a violent or turbulent background have a smaller hippocampus than individuals who have not been victims of their past. It is hypothesized that those who have smaller hippocampi are more likely to experience or induce unwanted flashbacks to stressful events. As a consequence of a weakened hippocampus, these individuals have difficulty putting memories in chronological order and suffer from short-term memory impairment.

Norepinephrine and cortisol are natural substances produced by your body that are responsible for improving your perception, reflexes, and reaction time in potentially dangerous circumstances. They also raise your heart rate, enhance the flow of blood and oxygen into your muscles and lungs, and prepare you to confront the challenges of life.

Whatever it is, you are going to have to suffer through it. While it is a false alarm, however, these surges continue to have an impact, and when you are not in immediate danger, the high amounts of chemicals and hormones that are flowing through your body have nowhere to go since they are not being used correctly. It is possible that you may become paralyzed as a consequence of this and will experience shaking, sweating, and being unable to breathe, among other physical symptoms. Can you picture going through all of this simply because you overthink or over worry about every little thing? When a single thought triggers an excess of stress-related sensations in your body, your body is going through a lot more than you would imagine. Fortunately, there are methods for reducing excessive worrying and developing habits that may help you is more productive in your daily life so that you don't slip into this vicious cycle.

HOW TO STOP WORRYING USING EFFECTIVE TECHNIQUES

Let's concentrate only on how to persuade you to put your worries aside. Keep in mind, however, that in order to manage with or completely eliminate anxiety, you will need determination, time, patience, and a great deal of work on your part. If you are constant and determined to train your anxious and disturbed mind, you will see some light at the end of your nightmare. However, it will not happen quickly. It doesn't matter how many "scientific" studies or research findings there are on what happens in the brain; the more you practice healthy habits to avoid falling into negative patterns, the more developed your brain will become, and eventually your mind will make new connections and instinctively handle worry-related situations in a productive manner.

Before we go any further, let's talk about cognitive distortions and why they might be difficult to get out of your thoughts. Having gained an understanding of why we are seemingly unable to bring ourselves out of our anxious condition, we can begin practicing the strategies with these distortions in mind.

To put it simply, cognitive distortions are illogical thinking processes that are caused by long-term habits and erroneous beliefs that we tell ourselves in order to cope with concerns or anxieties. However, we must recognize that these ideas—for example, you may believe you are unable to manage something when you are really capable—are just illogical and needless "comfort blankets" or "safety nets" that we construct in our brains to make us feel better. As a consequence, the individual falls into the mental trap of excessive worrying. Here are a few instances of cognitive illusions to think about:

• PERCEIVING SITUATIONS AS ALL-OR-NOTHING

This is a black-and-white way of looking at things. There is no such thing as a middle ground or a compromise. Someone has said that I am a failure, so it must be true.

Oversimplifying a situation:

Consider the possibility that one result will determine all others. As a result of my failure to get the position, I have concluded that I am unqualified and will never obtain employment.

• Constantly thinking negatively while avoiding thinking positively:

This occurs when you refuse to allow yourself to perceive the good parts of a situation and instead choose to concentrate only on the negative aspects. My brain must be completely devoid of brain cells since the only question I got incorrect was the final one.

• Concocting explanations for why favorable conditions in an occurrence are insignificant

Despite the fact that there were great things that occurred, you are aware of them and continue to create excuses for them. Despite the fact that I did an excellent job presenting myself in front of the employer, it is likely that they just had a good day and I will not get hired.

- **Making incorrect, pessimistic predictions, such as:**

You anticipate that something will occur in the future without any proof to support your claim. Whatever happens, I'm certain it will be horrible for everyone involved.

- **Being prepared for the worst-case scenario:**

You overstate the likelihood of events occurring or convince yourself that something terrible will occur. The train had arrived late. That must imply that something went wrong and that everything is now running behind schedule. The fact that I will be late for my appointment implies that I will be terminated from my position.

- **Opinions about what "should" and "shouldn't" be done or said**

When you don't follow your own views about what should and shouldn't happen, you beat yourself up. That was something I should have anticipated. I can't seem to get anything right.

- **Labeling YOU based on failures:**

You may think that I do not deserve a second opportunity since I generally do this because of anything you did wrong or because you failed yourself or someone else. I'm in tatters.

Assuming responsibility for something over which you have no control:

It's my fault that my grandmother's vase broke; I should have kept a closer check on my child and been more careful. So, why is it so tough to quit thinking about your worries? You may be completely unaware that you are indulging in these cognitive distortions. Many people begin to think this way long before the signs of excessive worrying or "disorders" show. You believe that worrying will help you solve a problem or prevent you from suffering unanticipated future events. Worrying, on the other hand, will not get you anywhere, and the only thing you can do is practice effective strategies to help you break away from this uncontrolled, negative thinking. Giving up worrying is crucial because it implies giving up the illusion that worrying serves a useful purpose.

How to Put an End to Your Worrying.

Worrying has been shown to cause more restless or sleepless nights, to assault your immune system, to increase your odds of having PTSD, and to increase your risk of dying at a younger age. The idea behind worrying, which creates so much distress, is that individuals cannot accept one basic truth: we have no control over some events in our lives. Most individuals worry because they either second-guess every choice or decision they make, or they can't accept that they don't have control, so they become perfectionists or "control freaks" to feel better about themselves. Is the drive to control or perfect everything, on the other hand, helping you felt well? If your response is no, consider the following methods for positive mind control:

1. Establish a "worry time"

Setting a defined time for when you can worry trains you to tell your fears that you don't have time right now, but that you will have time later to handle the issues. Make sure this "worry time" isn't shortly before bed or in the midst of a stressful activity, such as making supper. Make sure it is no more than an hour long. That way, you'll have plenty of time to address all of your concerns and devise effective solutions. Also, follow up your "worry session" with some meditation or deep breathing techniques.

RECOGNIZE THE CONCEPT OR ISSUE

If you have a concern that you can't get rid of throughout the day, write it down and acknowledge it. Trying to ignore or push the idea away will simply make it worse and "louder."

Accept that your concern may not be alleviated and move on. Don't spend too much time thinking about it; simply admit that it exists. When you're in your "worry time," go back through the notes you made during the day and evaluate them first.

MAKE A LIST OF THEM AND DISSECT THEM.

Maintain a journal. This works because when we attempt to think about our anxieties throughout the course of a busy day, we are more prone to thinking illogically or irrationally. When we express our anxieties in a notebook, we may not only vent, but we can also notice patterns in our thinking, allowing us to identify negative ideas and replace them with good ones. It also allows us to take a step back and look at our concerns as a whole, giving us a clearer idea of what to do next.

2. IMPROVE YOUR MINDFULNESS ABILITIES.

When you actively allow yourself to remain in the present moment, you are practicing mindfulness. It is to look at the red hues and count how many items are red in the room (or any other color). If you are drinking or eating anything, you should be entirely present with the taste, texture, smell, and appearance of the object. So, in a broader sense, when a concern emerges, don't pull it apart, don't criticize it, don't get nervous about it-just grasp that this worry is just a thought, and that's all it is. There is no action you need to take, no sentiments you need to attach to it, and nothing you need to do with this notion but be aware that it exists. If you are having difficulty doing this, get professional, therapeutic treatment or search for videos on the internet that will lead you through the procedure.

3. Exercise or Physical Activity

There have been many studies conducted all around the world, and practically everything you read suggests that mental health illnesses may be caused by the stomach. We have more energy when we consume better and healthier foods. When we have extra energy, we may find useful outlets for it, such as working out and exercising. From the comfort of your own home, go for a focused jog, a peaceful yoga session, or practice sit-ups and on-the-spot workouts like jogging in place, squats, and pushups. Enrolling in boxing lessons or joining a sport may be a smart choice. Furthermore, when you get your blood flowing and your pulse pounding, you have less mental energy to concentrate on the many problems that come into your thoughts, which helps you sleep better at night.

4. DETERMINE WHAT IS OUT OF YOUR HANDS.

This works best with the assistance of a therapist or a guidance counselor, but if you want to attempt it on your own for whatever reason, focus on what you can control and let go of what you can't. You cannot, for example, control someone else's conduct, but you can control how you respond to their words or actions. Recognize that, in most circumstances, you can only control how you respond or behave in situations or when confronted by someone else.

5. EVALUATE YOUR CONCERNS

When your concerns become too much, take a step back and look for the source of your concern. Most of the time, it arises from an apprehension that something bad may happen. Your phobias are frequently the result of unacknowledged anxieties. "Am I anticipating the future?" you should ask yourself. Do I have any doubts that I'll be able to manage whatever comes next? We often underestimate our ability to acquire control of ourselves and deal with problems. Sometimes you simply have to confront your anxieties, question your assumptions, and allow whatever occurs to happen. More often than not, you will discover that the situation was not as severe as you feared.

6. ENGAGE IN MEDITATION PRACTICE.

Meditation is one of the most efficient methods of relaxing. When we are comfortable, it is simpler for our brains to unwind and temporarily shut down. The majority of meditation focuses on our breathing. Meditation may teach you how to breathe properly, where to breathe from, and how to be more conscious of how you breathe while you're out and about. Although meditation may not provide instant comfort, I can tell you that it will make you feel more at ease in the long run. Meditation is not simply a short-term remedy for calming yourself down; it is a long-term, effective approach for teaching your mind to deal with stressful circumstances more effectively. A joyful, serene spirit comes from a peaceful, quiet mind. When our souls are at peace, our lives follow suit.

7. EMPLOY POSITIVE SELF-TALK.

When you have a nagging, nervous mind, it usually means you aren't giving yourself credit for previous bad situations. When you're scared, tell yourself, "I've gone through greater and worse situations than this before, therefore I'm quite capable of coping with what I'm feeling now." Replace your doubting thoughts with healthy affirmations for instant, in-the-moment relief. Whether you find yourself saying, "I'm not sure if I can do this," change it to, "I know I can." When you catch yourself thinking, "I hope he or she doesn't judge me," replace it with "I am confident" or "I am robust." Even if you don't believe the positive things you tell yourself, the longer and more often you think them, the more your mind will build these positive patterns of thinking, and the less likely your worries will be negative.

8. Let the true facts take the place of your worries.

When you start worrying about the past or the future, tell yourself that "all we have is now; I have no control over yesterday, and I have no means of forecasting tomorrow." The truth will assist you in being calm in the present moment by replacing your anxiety or fears with reality. Most of the time, we are distracted by things over which we have no control, making future forecasts or being too concerned with what is happening right now. When you're at a meeting and your mind begins to fret about how you're not going to be amazing or perform well, remind yourself, "Take a look at me. So far, I'm doing OK. If I make an error, I can and will be able to fix it. As a consequence of reinforcing positive thoughts and replacing them with facts, your concerns will diminish. Over time, you will be able to automate this procedure.

9. "WHAT IFS" DON'T MATTER; "HOW CAN I?" IS THE MOST IMPORTANT QUESTION.

As a result of anything like this, "Think about what may happen if you don't turn off the light and the house goes up in flames.

It's possible you're thinking, "What if I forget something?" Instead, think of this: how probable is it that my house will be destroyed by fire? There are a number of ways to deal with this lava lamp problem. If I forget anything, how will I be able to function? When you go from the words "what if" to "how can I," do you notice any differences? Most of the time, we obsess about hypothetical "what ifs" without any basis in reality.

10. BE OPEN TO THE UNEXPECTED.

We're all going to have to deal with the unknown at some point in our lives. Things that we can't control are like contemplating and worrying about things we can't control since we don't know. The number of individuals who feel the need to know everything and have a plan for everything is just too high. Develop a plan to just be. Just keep in mind that the unexpected might happen, so you should just have a positive outlook and not hold out much hope.

As a result, our anxieties are triggered by our concerns, which in turn lead to terror. As soon as we get nervous, we lose control of our rational thinking, which leads to a downward spiral of irrational thoughts. You'll feel less anxious and have more control over your surroundings and your own thoughts if you use these practical ways to stop worrying about things that aren't important.

Step Three: Refreshing Your Mind From A Negative Attitude

Having negative thoughts is akin to worrying and overthinking, except when you are just negative. Even if you're worried, it's the negative ideas you tell yourself that occupy the majority of your time and energy. Negative thinking and worrying both needs to be acknowledged in order to be dealt with. You can't simply wait for them to go away, push them away, ignore them, or pretend they aren't so horrible, as we discussed in the last chapter. Why? Why? Because they become worse. An unpleasant sibling will continuously poke you until you either snap or deal with the situation.

In other words, how precisely do you cope with negative thoughts? As long as you're aware of their presence, you can't ignore them. Dissect them to get to the root of the problem. Even if you strive to ignore something for as long as you can, it will either go away and return, or become more dominating and endure longer. If you tell yourself, "I'm not going to be like 'so and so,'" or "I'm never going to be or do 'whatever,'" and then do all in your power to avoid becoming or behaving like a particular person or even doing a certain chore, it may come full circle without you ever realizing it. As a result of this, you may find yourself doing or behaving in a way that you never intended to. This is how negative ideas function, so don't ignore them!

The best way to deal with bad ideas is to pay attention to them. Only by noticing your thoughts of "I'm not good enough and never will be" can you change them. Negative or good, it doesn't matter. Don't try to explain it or describe it. Just let it be. Just sit back and take it all in. Take some time to notice and experience this unpleasant notion, and then investigate it. So, take a look at what's going on in your personal and professional life. The fact that you've tried and failed to achieve things or acquire a job may be the root of your insecurities about your abilities. Determining why you didn't obtain the job you wanted may lead you to believe that your skills and abilities do not meet the requirements of the position. However, there may be other opportunities in the same sector. If

I need to, I can always look into other possibilities. "After you've observed, halted for a bit, recognized the thinking, and investigated why you'd think so, see how you feel. You'll most likely feel more productive and even better about yourself as a result of this.

Acceptance and Commitment Therapy (ACT) is the name given to what I just described (or ACT1). The beautiful thing about ACT is that you don't have to modify or dismiss your own ideas. As you can see, instead, you alter your perspective and behavior in response to them.

The ACT includes a number of minor actions you may take to reduce your negative thoughts:

REDIRECT YOUR ATTENTION TO SOMETHING UPLIFTING.

If you seek out hilarious sayings or memes, or converse with a positive person, your focus will be diverted from your negative thoughts. To prevent ignoring them, just shift your attention to anything else for a while. Instead of dwelling on the things that are bringing you down, focus on the things that are bringing you joy.

Self-love is a critical component in living a healthy lifestyle.

When you work and receive your paycheck, put 10% aside or utilize that 10% on anything for yourself, said someone close to me. I began doing this, and gradually I felt better. To the point that we forget to take care of ourselves because we're so focused on taking care of others, expenses, and food. To practice self-love, think of yourself as you would treat a close friend or a member of your family. When you find yourself dwelling on the bad, treat it as if it were coming from a trusted friend or family member.

Put an end to changing your activities or routines in order to make you feel better.

It's possible that you've developed an avoidance tendency as a consequence of your attempts to prevent your unpleasant thoughts from occurring. They are referred to as "intrusive thoughts" when your negative ideas appear out of nowhere or are provoked by external events. If, for example, you want to change your behavior, one of the following might be a good example:

If you have violent thoughts when you are near blades or while you are holding a knife, you may want to get rid of your knives or avoid touching them altogether.

If you have intrusive thoughts when you are around children, you may choose to restrict your involvement with them, be especially cautious about how you look at them, and even avoid changing or washing them altogether if necessary.

If any of these scenarios ring familiar, it's time to put an end to them. The more you feed into the fear of something bad happening as a result of your intrusive thoughts, the more they will take over and become more severe, potentially to the point where you will avoid leaving your house altogether. When you stop, you may discover that your ideas don't dominate you and they will go away on their own, since this is your method of "proving them wrong," in a sense. As a collection of words and phrases, your ideas will not compel you to do anything since they are only intended to cause confusion in your mind. Only you have the ability to choose what you will do with your actions.

WHAT HAPPENS IN THE MIND WHEN NEGATIVE THOUGHTS ARE INVOLVED?

In the Journal of Clinical Psychology, there was research centered on the consequences of anxiety and negative thoughts around a task. Participants were instructed to put objects into two groups. People who worried 50% of the time or more had a more difficult time categorizing the item into the two groups. This research reveals how negative thinking decreases the capacity to digest information as well as the ability to think effectively. This implies that thinking badly about issues doesn't help anything and might really make things more difficult owing to the confused thought-patterns around negative thinking.

Amygdala

The majority of the time, individuals is unable to regulate their negative thinking patterns, and this is due to the fact that the brain molds itself and evolves over time, dependent on the way we think and interpret certain things. As we learned in the last chapter, the amygdala is a part of the brain that stores bad memories and is in charge of the "fight, flight, or freeze" response when there is a threat.

Here's an excellent illustration of how the amygdala comes into play: Getting trapped in traffic may cause stress because of the amount of danger to one's safety, the fact that one is going to be late for work or to pick up someone, or the fact that there is a vehicle accident ahead. They don't see the "threat" as being really dangerous, but rather as an inconvenience from which they can quickly dispel any fears that something horrible is about to happen.

In contrast, for someone who has previously experienced stress related to traffic congestion, a vehicle accident, or any other unpleasant events related to this scenario, the amygdala will send signals to the body as if they were in fight or flight mode. Because of the accumulation of bad memories in the amygdala, this portion of the brain is unable to distinguish between false-alarm dangers and genuine threats, and as a result, it is sent into overdrive to protect us. This happens because negative thoughts are used over and over again for a long time.

THALAMUS

The thalamus is a part of the brain that is involved in the transmission of sensory and motor impulses. It transmits these signals to the rest of the body, but it is incapable of distinguishing between genuine danger and a false alarm in the process. The amygdala and the thalamus work together to either increase or decrease stress reactions in the rest of the body, depending on how you think or how well you manage your thoughts and emotions. True alarms are the result of your amygdala informing your thalamus that there is a threat. Once this happens, your thalamus transmits adrenaline signals to the rest of your body, preparing you to fight or run from the threat your brain has detected. It may appear out of nowhere and only occurs as a result of negative thought-patterns that have developed in your mind over time.

CHANGES IN CORTISOL

Cortisol is the stress hormone produced by your brain. It is in charge of controlling one's mood, motivation, and fear. Higher cortisol levels are associated with mental illnesses such as anxiety, depression, ADHD, post-traumatic stress disorder (PTSD), and other mood disorders. People who suffer from mental illnesses have greater cortisol levels than those who do not. As a result, it is far more difficult for these individuals to calm down. Their brains also include additional anomalies, such as abnormalities in the white and grey matter. In your brain, grey matter is where information is processed, and white matter is where your neurons link this processed information to the locations where it needs to go in your brain. Long-term stress, high cortisol levels, low dopamine and serotonin levels, and other things all cause the brain to make more white matter connections.

When white and grey matter are balanced in the brain, the regions of the brain responsible for mood and memory, such as the hippocampus, are left undisturbed, resulting in fewer "triggers" from the thalamus delivering false-alarm signals to the body, according to research. When you exercise positive thinking and break bad behaviors, you may bring about a balance between your white and grey matter.

This is how you would train your brain: by rewarding yourself for excellent conduct and developing self-discipline strategies, for example. In the case of dread of going alone to the shop, discipline yourself by traveling halfway to the store alone and chatting on the phone the remaining distance, while assuring yourself that you can do it and that it is not frightening. When you achieve tiny milestones toward your objective, reward yourself. This will ultimately lead to a large reward when you are able to walk to and from the shop by yourself.

REMOVAL OF TOXINS

The way you conduct your life has a lot to do with your tendency to think negatively. In order to cultivate positive thinking, you need to surround yourself with good influences. Negative thoughts and sentiments are more likely to arise when you are surrounded by poisonous individuals and places. Have you ever found yourself sitting there, tense for no apparent reason? Accepting that you're a tense person who can't unwind is one option. The poison in your life has become a routine for you. If you're not vigilant, toxicity may come from practically anywhere and everything. Being in a toxic relationship, renting from bad landlords, or working for terrible bosses isn't the only way to get you into trouble. You may also be best friends with toxic people. It doesn't matter what it is; you need to find out whether you are in a poisonous circumstance and make plans to leave it.

The following are seven things you can do to eliminate toxins from your life:

1. ANALYZE THE CIRCUMSTANCES AT HAND.

Analyze your current situation to locate the source of the poison and move forward from there. Determine when you were at peace, even if it was only for a short period of time. If so, where was it? What were your thoughts at this very moment, by the way? Where do you feel most at ease? What does it feel like to be in a state of inner harmony for you? How can this inner peace be achieved in your current circumstances, given where you are in life? It's important to find out what exactly it is about the person you're sharing a home with that is so bad, and how you can get rid of it. Whether the negativity is from your landlord's connection to you or from your own relationship with them, find out how you may break free of that attachment and move on. There is no time to waste in dealing with any kind of poison. Toxic fear will only grow if you put it off any longer.

2. NEGATIVE ITEMS SHOULD BE REPLACED WITH GOOD ONES.

A poisonous scenario may be replaced with a favorable one after you have discovered the problem. For example, if you feel overwhelmed at home and it is hard to find relief, then make it a practice to go for a run or do something pleasant for yourself every day. Get your favorite cup of coffee, or go to the beach with your dog for a day of relaxation. Going online to meet new people is a great way to escape harmful relationships in your current social group. If you find it difficult to meet new people, tell yourself that doing so will help you discover who you are and what you want to be. Try to look at the glass as half-full rather than half-empty. Perhaps your place of employment is the source of most of your anxiety. If so, consider searching for alternative employment or undertaking activities after work that satisfy your inner yearning.

3. FIND YOUR OR SOMEONE ELSE'S REASON FOR BEING.

Be thankful for what you have, no matter how little it seems to be. If you're surrounded by individuals who "suck the life" out of you because they are self-centered and don't support your aspirations, then you are not selfish. If you believe you're being taken advantage of, it merely shows that you have more empathy than you give yourself credit for, and you can empathize with yourself and others in order to see the bright side of things. When you awaken, consider yourself fortunate that you haven't become ill and aren't in the hospital. When you have a delicious dinner, remember to give thanks for the fact that you ate anything at all today. We tend to lose sight of the fact that there are many others who are going through considerably worse than we are. Even the tiniest things are taken for granted because we forget how fortunate we are. Consider yourself fortunate that you decided to acquire and could afford this book since it indicates that you are eager to learn and make positive changes. Be grateful for what you have since other individuals don't have the luxury of doing so.

4. FIND OUT WHAT YOU'RE PASSIONATE ABOUT AND WHAT YOU WANT TO DO WITH YOUR LIFE.

Because most individuals aren't living the life they deserve or enjoy, they tend to focus on negative thoughts and worry excessively. A life without passion is one in which you put up with a work environment or even a job you despise because it pays the bills. Consider the things you accomplish well that others find difficult. Do you have a knack with words? Do you have a strong grasp of language? Cooking is one of your strongest suits, isn't it? The place to begin is where you excel and where little effort is required. The reduction of poison will occur when you find your passion and strive to improve yourself, which will lead to self-compassion. When you're doing what you love, you won't care about anything else since it's something you look forward to doing.

5. REWARD YOURSELF FREQUENTLY.

Endorphins are the brain chemicals that make you feel happy. Dopamine is the brain chemical responsible for this. Dopamine is released when you reward yourself, no matter how tiny the gesture may seem. Good job. I woke up feeling glad for... I'm going to keep doing this, "is all you need to say to yourself when you feel grateful. Dopamine levels may be boosted by these self-talks, which establish a healthy habit of thinking positively. Enjoy a break as a treat in and of itself. It's a good idea to practice mindfulness when you're feeling overwhelmed or like you've lost control of your life. Focus on a pleasant emotion or recollection and live in the present now as if nothing else exists or matters. In the end, nothing matters more than your own happiness, so go ahead and do whatever it takes to get it. When you're in a good mood, everyone around you can feel it, too. Take frequent walks in nature to expose your brain to the sights, sounds, and fragrances of healing natural environments.

6. BE WILLING TO LEARN FROM YOUR ERRORS.

Keep reminding yourself that things aren't going to change right now. It's common for individuals to grow and improve their skills over time. Change isn't always as apparent as we'd want it to be. For example, I recall being pessimistic and unsure about my future. I began to make adjustments to my daily routine and the environment in which I lived. I changed my dietary choices, began taking daily walks, and became more conscious of my thoughts throughout the day. To combat negative thoughts, I paid attention to them and confronted them with truth and self-reflection whenever they surfaced. Rebuilding a feeling of belonging at home in my own house was the only way to get out of the circumstance that wasn't helping me. There was nothing strange about my former housemates until I went back to see them. They were still acting the same, but by then I'd noticed how much stronger and different my thinking was than it was when I was living with them.

As you can see, even though it is difficult and sometimes goes unrecognized, progress is made. Be patient with yourself and understand that you may have one, two, or even three poor days in a row since everyone has bad days. Recognize that the only way to improve is to learn from your failures. Instead of learning from our good habits, we learn from our errors because they teach us something new and remind us why we should build healthy habits.

7. Seek Expert Advice.

When nothing seems to be going right, you keep making errors, and you feel as if you have fallen more behind than when you began, seeking expert assistance may be the best course of action to follow. Therapeutic professionals such as psychologists, physicians, naturopathic practitioners, and clinical counselors may point you in the correct direction and teach you beneficial coping methods to get you started on the road to optimism. Often, anxiety or other mood problems take control of our thoughts, making it more difficult to get out of bed and have the desire to attempt every day to improve our situation. It is possible that the main issue is not your ideas, but something else entirely. Only a professional will be able to pull you out of your rut and get you on your way to achieving your goals.

We must eliminate toxicity from our lives since it may drag us down and drive us to think in a negative way even more often. Unless we eliminate or make an attempt to remove poison from our environment, we aren't giving ourselves a fair opportunity to succeed.

Step Four: In just a few minutes, you can learn how to stop overthinking and get rid of negative thoughts by following the steps in this article.

You might think of it as brain chatter or mental noise. Overthinking, worrying, and negative thinking all have this in common. These are the kinds of ideas that make it difficult to be at peace both within and outside ourselves. No matter what the scientific explanation is, it's all just mental clutter that accumulates over time. Often, it comes out of nowhere when we're stuck in a mental or physical rut and can't seem to get out of it, and it's usually uncontrolled. Using your ideas and mental chatter for positive purposes, such as preparation, research, and analysis, may be beneficial. Stress, anxiety, anger, and other unpleasant sensations are exacerbated when the thoughts do not have an off-switch.

We've already talked about what each of these mental chatter sounds means in previous chapters, but to help you remember, here's a quick recap:

- Negative thoughts or fears that have become habitual
- Replaying or repeating images or "movies" based on past memories or concerns;
- Fretting over the past or dreading the future, we lose sight of the here and now.
- When we can't stop thinking about the things we need to do, we can't concentrate on the discussion at hand.
- Perfection is our goal because we care about what other people think. As a result of our mental chatter, we are unable to accomplish the perfection we strive for.
- Daydreaming and irrational thinking it's because we are afraid of the future and can't control our thoughts that we worry too much about things we can't change.

Those who suffer from this sort of mental illness seem fatigued and worn out 90% of the time. Here, I'll show you how to train your mind to silence this kind of internal monologue. As a result, you'll be able to sleep better and enjoy some quiet time when you need it most. Concentration exercises are one of the most effective techniques to quiet the mind. As with all of the other methods described in this book, it will not happen immediately, but the more you practice, the quieter your mind will get. The ability to turn your mind on and off like a switch will eventually become automatic.

TAKING A BREATHER

It takes a lot of effort, persistence, and patience to learn how to calm your mind. Because peace of mind has so many benefits, it's important to cultivate it in your daily life. Finding inner peace will make it simpler to discover inner peace in every scenario and setting you encounter. In order to achieve inner peace and a tranquil mind, one must first overcome the limitations imposed by their own minds. The following are five tips for calming the mind and achieving inner peace:

1. Pay attention to the mental chatter that your ideas generate for you.

Do not assign labels to your ideas. As long as you don't criticize or identify an invasive, troubling thought like "I wish I were good enough" or "I want to damage myself," you may ignore it. Allow yourself to be aware of it. Make sure you don't push it away or avoid it by ignoring it. Let go of the past and accept the present as it is. When you do this, your ideas lose their ability to influence you, and you take back control of your life and your anxieties.

2. Intentionally and consciously question your own beliefs and assumptions.

Cognitive behavioral therapy is the basis of this method. Many psychologists swear by this technique since it allows you to rewire your brain to think in a different manner and develop new ways of interacting with your ideas. You regain control of the situation by confronting them head-on. To get started, think about what's going through your mind. To put it simply, if you're thinking that you aren't good enough, then ask yourself where this notion originates from. What do you mean by "jumping the gun?" What kind of cognitive distortion is this thought? Next, look for the good. You're not good enough because of anything that has occurred in your life, right? You might be able to get back in control of your thoughts if you find out where the idea came from and replace it with the truth.

3. Pay attention to your breathing.

When we're not breathing correctly, we're more likely to experience anxiety, worry, or even set off our "false alarm" mechanisms. Breathe in via your nose, mouth, or stomach, depending on where you're coming from. Observe your breath for a few minutes before moving on to the next step. Concentrate on taking in long, deep breaths after you've found out where and how your breath is coming from. To begin, take a five-second inhalation, hold it for three seconds, and then exhale slowly for five to seven seconds, counting each breath. When you're done, go back to normal breathing before you open your eyes again.

4. Music that soothes and inspires is an excellent way to help you relax and get in the right frame of mind.

One of the most effective ways to relieve stress is to listen to music. When we are able to identify with the singer, they become our favorite musician, and we feel more at ease knowing that they are singing about something that has personal significance to us. If you like instrumental music, pay attention to the tempo and the sound of the instruments themselves. Close your eyes and pay attention to any unnoticed sounds in the background. Attempt to identify the instruments and learn the song's lyrics.

5. be physically active on a regular basis.

Daily physical activity produces the "feel good" hormones we discussed before. Because our brains can more easily manufacture serotonin when dopamine is released, we experience a greater sense of well-being. Having a positive outlook on life reduces our stress levels and allows us to focus on the positive aspects of our lives. In order to keep our thoughts from overthinking or creating mental chatter, we need to engage in physical activity.

It's difficult to stop mental chatter from becoming worse when we overthink, worry, or think negatively all the time. In the next part, I'll go through ways to refresh your brain.

It's time to reboot your brain.

Resetting the brain is the greatest technique to get rid of negative thinking, worrying, and overthinking. In order to succeed, you must first be able to embrace change and conquer your own anxieties. Second, you must be open to learning new ways of thinking and changing your state of mind. Most importantly, how do we go about it? The majority of the "rebooting" procedure has previously been described. The other strategies, on the other hand, were designed to break the habit of overthinking. In today's world, there is more information to comprehend than there was three decades ago, and this is the fundamental reason most individuals have a hyperactive mind. Thanks to social media, technology, and the internet, we are constantly bombarded with fresh information. The goal of learning how to reset the mind, not how to halt or diminish your thoughts, is what you should keep in mind as you go through the following methods for rebooting your brain.

1. It's time to stop multitasking.

Even while multitasking has many advantages, it is also one of the causes of our brain's overactive state. This implies that our brains are constantly shifting our attention from one item to the next and then back again. Thinking in this manner really reduces one's capacity to do numerous tasks at once. No, I don't do that. I start with the dishes, then vacuum before they're done, then wipe the countertops and finish by sweeping or mopping the floors twice. For example, It's possible that you'll feel even more worn out than before after putting in that amount of effort. When you take a glance around, it seems as though you haven't done much: you still have clothes or dishes to do. Multitasking has this impact. In other words, the "squirrel effect" or "monkey brain" is what happens when you try to do too many things at once. Focus on one item at a time and make sure you don't move on to the next until that one job has been accomplished before moving on to the next.

2. Keep your focus on a single task at a time.

Daniel Levitin, the author of The Organized Mind: Thinking Straight in the Age of Information Overload, advocates Deliberate Immersion. Our jobs or obligations should be broken up into 30- to 50-minute blocks of uninterrupted time so that we may focus only on the work at hand. According to Daniel Levitin, our brains are made up of two types of intentional networks: task-positive and task-negative. Being able to complete tasks without being distracted by the outside world or the surroundings, such as watching television or conversing with loved ones in your home or having your phone ringing and bringing up social media or what's going on outside your home, is an important skill for anyone who works from home. Whenever your attention is diverted from the activity at hand, you are engaging in the negative-task network. As a result, you are unable to accomplish a task since your mind is elsewhere. Inspiration and creativity come from bad tasks. An "attention filter" is then responsible for switching between the modes. It keeps us organized and allows us to concentrate on the task at hand, helping us to do it more quickly.

3. The "Attention Filter"

Therefore, if you want to be more creatively productive, Daniel Levitin recommends scheduling time for social interactions while working on a subject that requires concentration or attention. Status updates, Twitter, SMS messages, figuring out where you left your wallet, and other such activities have their proper place and time. A wonderful technique to refresh the brain is to concentrate on one subject at a time and not be distracted by other things, such as social media, during that time. When you're taking a stroll in the woods, listening to music as you check your social media, or taking a bath while you read a book, you're engaging in task-negative networking (daydreaming, mind wandering, or deep pondering). Our minds are reset when we engage in mind-wandering activities like these. As a result, we get new perspectives on what we are doing or planning to do.

MINDFULNESS IS COMPRISED OF FOUR STEPS.

In the present moment, mindfulness is an excellent means of resetting the brain's internal clock. You may return to mindfulness if you find yourself experiencing "squirrel" moments or having difficulty shutting off the "monkey mind." The practice of mindfulness may assist with more in-depth relaxation methods such as meditation, sleep, and focus. The following are the four stages to successfully practicing mindfulness:

Relabel

Relabeling is the process of taking a step back and dealing with the concept, emotion, or action. Consider the following question: Under which cognitive distortion does this thinking fall? Which emotion do you think you can associate with this thought? What do you feel compelled to do as a result of this thinking and feeling? Why? As soon as you recognize these communications, you'll be able to determine where they're coming from and whether or not they're "false alarms."

Reattribute

Once you have discovered the message that your thought, emotion, or action is bringing to the surface, you must reassign the notion to a new point of view in order to go forward. By analyzing it, you can determine how essential the notion is to you. If it is significant or repeated, consider adding a new meaning to the back of it and seeing it from a fresh perspective.

Refocus

After you have addressed the idea, pulled it apart, given meaning to it, and altered your view, you should shift your attention to another topic. The goal of this is to avoid being trapped in your thoughts about it for an extended period of time, since this is what causes your brain to become hyperactive and scattered. Rewiring and rebooting your brain occurs when you deliberately shift your attention away from one subject and toward another.

Revalue

When you have mastered the first three processes, you may go on to the revaluing step. After a period of time, it occurs virtually instantaneously. Revaluing implies that you are able to recognize your ideas, feelings, and impulses for what they really are. As soon as you recognize these things for what they really are, you will have reset your brain, allowing it to reconfigure and arrange your ideas in the appropriate "brain slots." Your brain will be able to determine if a thought or message is good or damaging on its own.

Briefly stated, the quickest and most effective method of rebooting the brain is to refrain from multitasking, recognize when you are juggling too many tasks or taking on too much information, switch from negative thinking about things to positive thinking about things, be mindful of your thoughts, and practice paying attention to only one thing at a time.

"Paralysis in the Analysis"

Analysis paralysis, also known as paralysis by analysis, is an opposing pattern that refers to the condition of over-analyzing (or overthinking) a problem to the point that no choice or action is taken, hence paralyzing the result.1

I prefer to think of it in terms of the "flight, fight, or freeze" response, with analytical paralysis being the freeze reaction. The term "solution paralysis" refers to when a person becomes so engrossed in their own ideas about what to do with a problem solution that they are unable to choose which solution to take, and so they do nothing. Analysis paralysis is caused by a lack of decision-making abilities. According to Herbert Simon, a psychologist from the United

States, humans make judgments in one of two ways:

Satisfice

This means that people choose the option that best meets their needs or catches their eye.

Maximize

People are unable to be satisfied with just one option, and instead develop a number of alternatives, always feeling that there are better possibilities than their original pick. Maximizes are the ones that are most prone to suffering from analytical paralysis. The reason people overthink is because they are afraid of making errors and want to prevent the danger of failing. Analysis paralysis is a fancy term for not being able to make decisions because of too much overthinking and deliberation.

ANALYZING THE SITUATION PARALYSIS

Because analysis paralysis is caused by a lack of capacity to make good and timely judgments, the most effective strategy to overcome it is to simply improve your decision-making abilities. Here are some strategies for getting unstuck when you've been too analytical to the point of analysis paralysis:

1. Establish a hierarchy of importance for your choices.

Make a list of your choices and categorize them, which mean you should determine which decisions are major and which are minor, which decisions are critical and which ones do not need much attention. When deciding which decisions to categorize into which categories, ask yourself the following questions:

- How critical do you think this choice is?
- How pressing is the decision I need to make? What is my time frame?
- Is it likely that this choice will have a significant or little influence on what occurs next?
- Based on the solutions I've come up with, here are some of the best and worst-case scenarios:

When we group our options, it makes it easier for us to stick to our decision and not change our minds later on in the process.

2. Include the "end aim" in your solution as part of your overall strategy.

Getting caught in the analysis-paralysis trap occurs when you are unable to determine why you need to make a choice in the first place. There are numerous additional ideas that might influence our judgments, such as "What if I make the incorrect choice?" or "There are so many things I can do, but which is the best choice to make?" In the event that you do not understand why you must make a choice, in this instance, identifying the purpose or target may be a more effective method of approaching the situation. Consider the following scenario: You are caught between two professions. You already have a career in which you are successful, but you want to try something new and you are confused about why you need to make a choice or even if you should. Ask yourself what your ultimate goal is-where do you believe you should or will be in five to 10 years' time? When you think about the "ultimate goal," it may be easier to figure out what you need to do.

3. Break down your options into smaller time chunks.

Essentially, this strategy is the polar opposite of the previous technique. Your attention remains focused on your ultimate objective, but, rather than taking action in response to this objective, you are breaking your ultimate objective down into smaller objectives. Once you've made a decision, you can divide it into smaller decisions to achieve the "mini goal(s)."While you are still in the process of making a choice, be certain that when you make a final decision, you stick to it. If you are still having trouble selecting, jot your options down on a piece of paper and limit yourself to no more than three to five choices. Eventually, the more you do this, the smaller the list will grow each time, and you will only have to make one choice, which is a goal in and of itself-overcoming analysis paralysis-as a result of your efforts.

4. Obtain a second opinion

If you are still confused after making your list and you are still overthinking the many options available to you, then choose two of the most promising alternatives and present them to a trustee for consideration. Allowing yourself to do so will allow you to let go of any judgments. Allow yourself to let go of control and perfectionism. Rely exclusively on this other person's perspective, and if they provide you with counsel on a choice you are still unclear about or may not have selected in the end, remind yourself that you came to them because you were struggling and that you trust their judgment and recommendations. Consider how many times you may have been wrong about this individual when you went against them in the past. Deliberately reminding yourself that you need to let go of the dread that something horrible may happen is also beneficial. According to a saying that has had a significant influence on me and the people in my life, insanity is doing the same thing over and over again and expecting different results. 2. Or, to put it another way, if you continue to do the same thing while expecting a different result, the change will never materialize.

Fear

Overthinking, worrying, and other forms of negative thinking are all fueled by a single emotion, which is fear. Common fears include fear of losing control, fear of making a mistake or failing, fear of making a choice, or simply a general sense of dread. These are all common fears. Fear is something that can be learnt and overcome through self-discipline and exposure treatment. A person's fear can paralyze them and prevent them from doing what they want, resulting in them missing out on potentially lucrative opportunities. Fear is the most common reaction to excessive worrying and overthinking on the part of the brain. For us to be in complete control of our thoughts and actions, we first need to face and overcome our fears.

Here are some strategies for dealing with your fears:

1. Acknowledge that the fear (no matter how great or tiny) is genuine.

When individuals experience dread or are apprehensive about a certain item or a range of things, the fear is genuine to them. Fear is frequently a wonderful thing to experience; it signifies that our human instincts are operating correctly. For example, a lady who is going home after work in the dark by herself should have anxieties or fears about walking alone in the dark. A kid's first day of school may be worried and frightened, as well as a youngster or student who starts a new school in the midst of the year. A guy who has to go into surgery on his brain or another working organ, or a person who has to go to the dentist, both dread the possibility of a poor result. These are all anxieties that should be there. However, a fear of clowns, tiny places, flying, or heights is all illogical fears or anxieties that have been learnt. Whatever someone fears is true to them and should be treated with respect rather than being pushed to conquer. Fears cannot be conquered unless the individual is determined to handle them.

ACCEPT YOUR TREPIDATION.

Accept the fact that you have this phobia. This might be anything as significant as beginning a new career, meeting new people, relocating to a new town or city, or becoming a parent. Another example is a spider scurrying across your foot, strange creaking sounds in your new home, someone frightening you, or even driving while frightened. If you are afraid of anything, acknowledge that this is the fear you are experiencing; do not try to avoid or reject it. It's there, and you're terrified of it.

BREAK IT DOWN INTO SMALLER PARTS.

Take a step back and look at your fear with fresh eyes. Consider the following questions:

- At what level of danger are you?
- Is it possible that experiencing this dread will be harmful to you?
- When your worst fear comes true, what do you think will happen?
- What are the best and worst-case scenarios if you were confronted with this fear right now, at your leisure?

Fears might be unreasonable, causing many individuals to overthink their decisions at times. Other times, overthinking leads to the development of new worries. So, after you've answered those questions for yourself go ahead and ask some more:

- What would you do if the worst-case situation occurred? What would you do if the worst-case scenario occurred?
- Do you think you'll be able to manage the situation? Do you believe you will?

- If the situation occurred (in the best-case scenario), what would you do to avoid it?
- ·Do you place too much faith in your capacity to deal with the situation? Often, individuals have the same worries as one another. Find someone with whom you can talk about your fears and work together to get over them.

When you have the same worries as someone else, you have a feeling of belonging because you know that you are not alone in your anxieties and concerns.

4. Give in to your fears and brace yourself for the worst.

The most effective method of overcoming your worries is to confront them or to pay close attention to them. In the beginning, being out in public gave me a lot of fear. As a result, when confronted with a public scenario, such as grocery shopping, I would get overwhelmed and experience bodily symptoms of terror, similar to those experienced during a panic attack. As soon as I made the conscious decision to go out in public, I began by observing my thoughts and, if they were negative, challenging them and replacing them with more positive ones. Whenever my fear got too much for me, I would return home and try again the following day, after I had regained some control over my emotions. I didn't allow fear to take over because

I was determined to fight back. This is referred to as "exposure treatment" in certain circles.

Exposure Therapy is a kind of therapy in which a person is exposed to something for a period of time.

Exposure therapy does not work for everyone, but if you commit yourself to continuing to attempt it even when fear takes over, you will be able to overcome the same thing you are scared of in the long term. The use of exposure treatment is something a psychologist would recommend to someone suffering from panic disorder or another kind of mood illness. It is a sort of treatment that assists individuals who are suffering from mood disorders in confronting their unjustified anxieties. Exposure therapy, on the other hand, does not need the presence of a handicap in order to be effective; it may be used by anybody who is eager to learn. There are many different forms of exposure therapy, including the ones listed below:

EXPERIMENTATION IN VIVO

This is the act of confronting a dreaded item, circumstance, or action in real-life situations head-on. For example, someone who is afraid of public transportation may be recommended to take a bus or a monorail instead (first with someone, then without someone). Someone who is uncomfortable with social contact may be advised to begin by delivering a speech in front of a small group of people before progressing to a larger audience.

EXPOSURE IN ONE'S IMAGINATION

Then you sit with a trusted friend or psychotherapist and allow them to visually walk you through your frightened item, circumstance, or action. For example, a person suffering from post-traumatic stress disorder (PTSD) may go through a guided visualization of the things that have occurred to them that revolved around their anxiety from the past. Over time, their dread begins to have a less negative impact on them.

EXPERIMENTING WITH VIRTUAL REALITY

When alternative exposures are neither practicable nor beneficial, virtual reality may be utilized to supplement the experience. Someone who is afraid of flying, for example, may choose to engage in a virtual or guided vision of flying. This virtual world takes the user into the world of flight without them having to actually fly. It lets them experience the sights, sounds, smells, and textures of their surroundings.

INTERCEPTIVE EXPOSURE IS DEFINED AS

This is the practice of purposefully causing the bodily feelings associated with the dreaded experience to occur. Someone suffering from a panic condition, for example, may experience increased terror when they get dizzy as a result of a panic episode. In order to emphasize the effects, they may be encouraged to spin in circles before attempting to stand, maintain their balance, or even sit down. This is done in order for kids to comprehend that the physical impacts are not as frightening while they are occurring since they can replicate the same sensations for themselves. Exposure therapy aids in the treatment of phobias by developing and rewiring the brain to form new neural connections that are more effective. When people deliberately make or face their fears, the dread just fades away and has no effect on the person who is feeling it.

STEP FIVE: USING POSITIVITY

As with negative thinking, the issue with positive thinking is that it is just as infectious as negative thinking. In other words, when you are in the presence of a positive person, you might absorb their "vibe" or energy and become more optimistic yourself. It has an impact on more than just yourself; it has an impact on the people and environment around you. Consider the following scenario: If you were to go to a job interview and come in with a confident and cheerful attitude, the company would be more likely to hire you. If you arrive at work fatigued, hungry, or overworked, your mood will reflect this, and you will not be able to put your best foot forward in the meeting or presentation. The company would most certainly turn a blind eye to your situation and hire the next good candidate that showed up for an interview instead. It's as simple as this: what draws positive also attracts positive, and vice versa.

As previously described in the preceding chapters, it has been shown that the shape and structure of our brains may vary based on how we think and conduct our lives. What's more remarkable is that when we repeat habits, beliefs, and actions over and over, we are really teaching our brains to do so. As a result of doing things over and over, our brains form new synapses that were not previously there, and these new synapses get associated with actions, resulting in the development of new habits. As a result, it is reasonable to assert that when we think negatively, we are essentially repeating negative ideas to ourselves. While our brain makes connections between negative thoughts and the activities that we engage in, we continue to engage in poor habits as a result. This is something we can accomplish with positive thinking as well. Have you ever heard the expression, "Life is what you make it."? This is true owing to the fact that when we incorporate negative ideas, we act, perceive, feel, and engage in bad behaviors as a result of those thoughts. When we repeat positive statements to ourselves (even when we don't believe them), we begin to see, hear, think, and act in ways that are more positive.

The reason negativity is prevalent in this generation or in our culture is that negativity is very addicting in nature. It's difficult to break free, and once we start thinking badly, we can't stop because it has the effect of a narcotic. The reason we do these things is because we don't want to accept responsibility; instead, we prefer to place the blame on our negative thoughts as the reason we are melancholy. We attribute our feelings of anxiety to our excessive worrying. We attribute our behaviors to our tendency to overthink things. It's a difficult thing to swallow, but the only one who can be held responsible for your bad thoughts is YOU. The problem is that change is difficult. That which we continue to do, that which we are used to, is what is simple. Thus, it's no surprise that we don't just wake up one day and declare, "Hey, I'm going to be optimistic today." But there is a solution; it is up to you to choose to wake up and be optimistic, and it is really as simple as that. What is difficult, though, is continuing to try something new and unusual. It's so important that if you really want to get out of the nightmare of negativity that has been your life, you must be willing, willing, or even desperate to change and change your brain in a more positive direction.

How To Keep A Positive Attitude Throughout Your Life

More than just what you are thinking about when you learn to think positively and improve your capacity to do so, practicing positive thinking contributes to your happiness when you practice positive thinking. It takes on the features of the environment in which it is placed. It becomes a part of your own identity as a result of this experience. Positivity, like negativity, has the power to consume us and consume us completely. When everything and everyone around you seems to be negative or worrisome, it may be difficult to maintain an optimistic outlook on a terrible day. When you think positively, your aura and mind stop looking for the bad in every situation, and you begin to feel thankful for the tough days and serious failures that have occurred since they have helped to shape your present and future. No matter how bad a situation seems to be, there is always something good to be taken away from it. At first, identifying the positive aspects of a situation may seem difficult, but with time and practice, it will become so instinctive that you will no longer have to think about it; the positive aspects of a situation will just be there for you to observe. So, what is the most efficient method of accomplishing this goal? Four ways to boost your degree of optimism in your daily life are as follows:

1. Make a point of focusing on three (or more) good things every day.

Before you go to sleep at night, go through your day in your head again and again. Consider everything that occurred and write down three good impressions that you gained from the day. Anything might be the case. Was the sun shining brightly? Have you reconnected with an old acquaintance? Perhaps your supervisor or a coworker wasn't quite as grouchy today, which resulted in a less stressful day overall. The more you begin to notice the minor positive benefits, the more your sense of positivity will grow, and the sooner you will experience pleasure and success as a result of those small positive effects.

2. Do something pleasant for a stranger if you can.

Although it may not appear so, acts of kindness have the power to lift not only your spirits but also the spirits of those around you. When we perform good deeds for others, we are really nourishing our own souls with happiness because the chemical endorphins released in our bodies work as a reward response in our brains. They might be anything from a simple smile to doing something considerate for a stranger to taking the time to do something thoughtful for a loved one, among other things. Making someone else happy makes your heart smile, which in turn makes you feel better about yourself and helps you grow in confidence.

3. Keep your attention on the present moment.

If I haven't said it enough times, I'll say it again: be cautious of your surroundings! When we remain present in the present moment, it brings balance and structure to our own awareness of what is going on in the world around us. By being aware of our surroundings while remaining in the present moment, we will be able to notice the wonderful things that happen more readily, while negativity will seem to be a distant acquaintance.

4. Demonstrate gratitude and self-acceptance.

The thing about optimism is that it makes it easy to assist others and give something back to the universe when you love yourself. Just think about it: if you don't value and appreciate yourself, your relationships will suffer, your career will be unfulfilling, and you will continually doubt your capacity to deal with pressure. Being grateful for what you have is possible when you love yourself. Envy or jealousy no longer appears to be something to be concerned about, and you won't feel the need to beg for more of what you don't have. To be thankful for whom you are as a person, you must first accept yourself and get a clearer vision of your life's goals. If you have the opportunity, focus on being thankful rather than envious of others. The grass isn't always greener on the other side of the fence.

ADAPTING TO A NEW ATTITUDE

When we're in a bad mood, we're more likely to become trapped in a rut of negative thinking. Overthinking (or negative thoughts) leads to a vicious cycle: unpleasant moods are brought on by worrying thoughts, which in turn prompt us to worry about additional negative consequences, which makes it difficult to make crucial choices since our brains are so cluttered. We all have days when we don't want to get out of bed, but we also have days when we're energized and able to do more. Reflect on your most productive days and attempt to draw from that energy when you're feeling down, nervous, or sad. If you find yourself in a bad mood, it's OK to succumb to it, but don't let it become a regular routine.

When you're mired in the mud, here are some methods to lift your spirits:

1. Participate in some physical activity.

We've previously spoken about this topic as well. When you exercise, those "feel good" chemicals in your brain are released, which has the ability to instantaneously alter your mood. Additionally, it is an excellent way to divert your attention away from your negative mood since, rather than concentrating on what caused you to be sad, you may divert your attention to other things, like the landscape or your breathing. It is important to drink enough water when working out since being dehydrated can actually make you feel worse.

2. Obtain uplifting content by listening to or watching it.

It's okay to watch an inspirational movie or listen to an uplifting podcast on days when you don't feel like moving or getting out of bed. It's just one of those days, after all. Even if we have a tendency to listen to music that corresponds to how we are feeling in our bad times, we should resist this impulse and instead play some joyful, optimistic music instead. Who knows, it could even try to compel you to dance or sing in response. When compared to listening to or watching negative or sad material, listening to or watching encouraging material will lift your spirits 60% faster. Strangely enough, when we listen to music that matches our current mood, we are really training our brains to accept these attitudes as normal, and we find ourselves sliding further into the negative cycle as a result of this training.

3. Modify your physical demeanor.

This implies that you should act and behave in the manner in which you want to be felt. So, if you want to feel more confident, dance about the house in the sexiest or wackiest outfit you own and stand in front of a mirror with your chest pushed out and your back straight to achieve this. If you want to feel calm, put on your most comfortable clothing and lay about, but be cautious of what you tell yourself while doing so. I promise that if you force yourself to grin for 60 seconds, your mood will improve, even if it is just a little. Don't allow negativity to overtake you; instead, choose to be yourself. To get out of the funk you are in and into the mood you want to be in, try being humorous, laughing, tickling yourself, talking to someone about your hopes and dreams, or doing anything else that will help you to feel better.

4. Show gratitude or appreciation for everything in your life. 5.

Here's a strange and amusing fact: when someone goes about complaining about everything, we consider it normal to ignore them. We sit and listen to our friends vent, our parents argue, our employers grumble, and even strangers debate with themselves at times, all of which we find entertaining. We are used to hearing people moan and argue about their problems, but wouldn't it be strange to hear someone express their gratitude and appreciation for all they have in their lives? The phrases "It's pouring outside, and I am so glad for the rain" and "Meal is sometimes taken for granted; I just wanted to take a minute to feel fortunate for this food" are heard all the time, don't you think? Have you ever heard someone say something like, "I enjoy that my children yell and act out because it shows they are developing as human beings"? No, it's likely that you haven't. Consider what would happen if you shouted out loud everything you were thankful for today, everything you enjoyed today, and everything you appreciated yesterday. Consider how you would feel and how you would make others feel if you were in this situation. You could even have a nice chuckle, but isn't that what it's all about anyway? This is something you should practice.

5. Maintain your positive attitude even when you don't feel like it.

The reality of your ideas is that they do not have the ability to govern your actions. This is also true of emotions; they do not have authority over you. So, if you're having trouble exercising or enforcing the strategies you've learned so far, simply go ahead and do it. Force yourself to smile, force yourself to get out of bed and dance, and force yourself to be thankful for what you have. Take charge of your surroundings and your actions as you get out of bed in the morning and inject some optimism into the world. This tells your brain that even when you're in a bad situation and feeling down, you can choose how you respond. This leads to more optimism and good behavior.

CREATING AND REINFORCING POSITIVE HABITS

When it comes to developing a happy attitude on a consistent basis, just thinking positively and altering your mood isn't enough. It is necessary to establish habits in order for your brain to cease synapsing the negative enforcement you have established and begin synapsing the good enforcement. While the preceding workouts will be effective in the short term, you will need to not only do them on a regular basis, but also develop good daily habits in order to see long-term results. Maintaining good behavior over time can help you become less nervous, less of a "worry wart," and more laid-back in your approach. When you see that you are no longer nervous throughout the day and that you can find the silver lining in any event, you know you have succeeded in being positive. You will have clarity of thought and acceptance of what you cannot control, which means that you will have accepted that negativity no longer consumes you since you have regained control. Let's take a look at some of the ways you might develop good habits in order to experience these wonderful outcomes:

1. Identify the source of the problem.

Beginning to deal with the source of your negativity is just the beginning of the work that needs to be done before you can go on with your day. Consider (but don't dwell on) the reasons why you may be in a poor mood or where your negative thoughts are coming from (but don't overthink it). Instead of focusing on your bad thoughts as a result of continuous behavior around this particular concept, it may be more straightforward to shift your focus to anything someone else said to you to help you get yourself in a better mood. Once you've identified the source of the negativity, it will be much simpler to choose what to do next to combat it.

2. Begin each day with a positive attitude.

Get out of bed and be grateful for your life. Be grateful for your children, your spouse, or even the fact that you are not homeless at this time. Keep being thankful for your friends and family, but most of all, keep being thankful that you are alive and that you have gotten yourself to where you are in life right now! Do one thing every day when you wake up that will make you feel better and improve your mood. Make a practice of doing one thing you didn't get around to doing yesterday. Getting out of your comfort zone and starting the day with optimism is essential if you want to see progress. This might be anything from listening to your favorite music to preparing your favorite meal to taking a thoughtful stroll or jog. Always remember to begin and end your day with positive affirmations for yourself, such as, "This is going to be a fantastic day," or, "Today was fantastic, and tomorrow will be even more fantastic."

3. Keep a sense of humor during difficult times.

If you are having a difficult day or are confronted with a negative influence or situation, then make an inner joke about it to cheer yourself up (to yourself, preferably). In fact, you may discover that you are more amusing than you realize, and it is a wonderful way to make light of a terrible situation. Rather than calling your spouse vulgar names during an argument, consider what would happen if you called them something more appropriate, such as fruitcake or wheelbarrow. Consider their faces to be the shape of a tomato or a car wheel. Instead of swirling in a spiral of negative ideas, imagine your mind spinning in a whirlwind of humorous recollections. Perhaps you've just lost your job, and instead of worrying about the financial strains or all of the bad things that are likely to happen, consider how wonderful it would feel to have a few days (or weeks) to yourself to recharge your batteries. Consider how your future job will be better than the one you have now, and consider how ambitious you are in general.

4. Look at each setback as an opportunity to learn and grow.

Rather than being afraid of making errors, you could experiment by purposefully creating mistakes to see what occurs. Some of your blunders may not only teach you what not to do or what to avoid in the future, but they may also provide you with insight into the fact that things aren't quite as horrible as you had previously assumed. Most importantly, when you make a mistake, use the opportunity to learn from it. If you make a mistake at work, such as getting documents jumbled up or names mixed up, just apologize and make a mental note to double-check your work the next time. Perhaps you forgot a buddy's birthday, and it happens to be your dearest friend, whom you will always remember. It is possible that they are not experiencing the same level of distress that you are, so don't be too hard on yourself about it. Instead, make a note of it in your calendar for next year and see yourself doing something really extraordinary for them (not just on their birthday, but any day of the year as well).

5. Negative ideas should be replaced with positive ones.

Some individuals are used to negative thinking, and it might be difficult to catch them in a bad mood when they are at their worst. Nonetheless, if you do find yourself thinking things like, "I'm terrible at this," or "I never do anything correctly," purposefully make a mental note of them and then just replace them with anything else. Instead, think, "I may be awful at something, but with practice I will become better. Therefore, I must not give up since I am capable of doing this," or, "Just because it seems like I never do anything properly, does not always imply that this is true; I am excellent at many things." When you intentionally replace negative ideas with more positive ones, you are recognizing your negative thoughts and establishing a habit of thinking more positively. It's OK if you don't believe in yourself at first, but you'll notice a difference in your mood after doing this consistently for a few times.

6. Refrain from getting involved in drama.

Humans have always been drawn to drama, but when we get entangled in the gossip and dramatic twists of our own or another's life, the results may be quite detrimental. As soon as we stop paying attention to these sorts of occurrences, we can begin concentrating more on our own lives and doing more productive tasks. Drama may be found in movies or on television, but try to stay away from drama in other people's lives, or even in your own.

7. Rather than creating new problems, concentrate on finding solutions.

Problems are what put you in this situation in the first place. We are attempting to solve issues in order to prevent them. Problems may be resolved by asking more questions and being more involved in the issue. Instead of being in your brain, try to be completely in the moment. You will be better prepared to deal with any issue or charge that comes your way. Keep your cool and think logically or creatively. Listen to your gut instincts rather than your hyperactive head. Give yourself (or the person or event) a couple of days to think about something before making a choice. Problems should be written down, and solutions should be "thought mapped." Create an effort to come up with no more than three solid options before moving on to the section of this book that covers how to make decisions (in the next chapter). This is the only way you will be able to properly resolve your issues.

8. Go through the process again.

This is the last and most straightforward step: just keep repeating it. When you find you overthinking, overly worried, or seeing your negative thoughts assaulting you again, go back to the beginning of this list and start from the beginning. Restart the process. Make an effort to do this every day and complete these steps completely with your full attention focused on them. If you perform this correctly, you will notice a favorable change in your life and the development of new surroundings inside of you. You will gradually but steadily change your negative attitude and habits, and optimism will become your natural state of mind and be a habit for you.

Step six: Learn how to declutter your mind and become the person you want to be in life.

A Short brief of this chapter: You will learn how to get enough sleep, and stay asleep, so you have the energy to stay focused on being positive, developing self-confidence, improving your decision-making skills, stopping procrastination, starting to set goals, and learning more techniques on how to effectively solve problems. Perhaps this chapter is the most essential chapter you have come across yet. So let's go right in.

- Low energy (regardless of what you do);
- Difficulty concentrating on anything;
- Irritation or other mood changes;

- Reduced performance at work and school due to thought patterns and lack of sleep;

There are many distinct sorts of insomnia; let's have a look at some of them right away: **I had insomnia for a short period of time.**

This sort of sleeplessness is dependent on the circumstances. Take, for example, if you are having trouble sleeping because of a test you are dreading, a presentation you aren't fully prepared for, or an event you have been looking forward to for months.

INSOMNIA OVER A LONG PERIOD OF TIME

You are experiencing sleep disruption when you are unable to remain asleep after having fallen asleep for a period of time. This happens at least three times a week and lasts for around three months or more, depending on the individual.

INSOMNIA WITH COMORBIDITY

As a result of the presence of anxiety, depression, or other psychological problems, this condition is emphasized.

INSOMNIA THAT BEGINS RIGHT AWAY

This is the stage during which you may have difficulty going to sleep, regardless of the underlying reason.

Insomnia on a Regular Basis

At this stage, you are able to fall asleep, but you are having difficulty remaining asleep throughout the night. It is getting more difficult to fall asleep again. When someone suffers from insomnia, it may cause significant disruption in their lives in a variety of ways.

However, with the right mindset and the appropriate drive, it is possible to correct the situation.

What You Can Do to Improve Your Sleeping Habits

If you experience any of the symptoms listed above, or if you have been diagnosed, the following are some suggestions to help you sleep better:

1. Create a sleep schedule.

If you're not sure how to go about it, think about how you would put your baby, toddler, or children to sleep if you were in their shoes. It usually begins about an hour before bedtime when you switch off the electronics, after which they take a bath, have a small snack, and drink a glass of water, after which it's pajama time, story time, and finally, finally, goodnight. You may find that some children like it when you hug them, or just touch their backs, or sing to them. Prepare for sleep by creating a personal nighttime ritual that begins about an hour before you plan to sleep. By doing this on a regular basis and adhering to it, you will make it simpler for that mental noise to subside and you will be able to relax more easily.

2. Participate in regular physical activity sometimes,

The reason it is so difficult to fall asleep is that our bodies have stored up a great deal of energy. The reason for your restless leg syndrome is that your legs need to be stretched out and massaged more often. Exercise is excellent for helping the body relax later in the day, whether you do it first thing in the morning or approximately two hours before you want to sleep.

2. Keep technology to a minimum.

One of the most important reasons is that technology, such as televisions, phones, and other electronic gadgets, emits blue light, which our brains interpret as "daytime." As a result of this blue light, our brains create less melatonin (a hormone that helps us sleep), and our brains gradually lose the ability to distinguish between night and day. So turn off your gadgets, unless you're listening to breathing exercises or guided meditations, in which case keep them on.

4. Set up your bed solely for sleeping or intimacy.

Because you use your bed for nearly everything, it may be difficult to remain asleep or fall asleep at night. Do you like to eat in your sleep? Visiting with buddies while lying on your bed? Does your bedroom serve as a place where you make phone calls? Is there a television set in your room? If so, what channel is it? All of these factors might lead the brain to believe that your bed is more like a sofa and that your room is more like a living room than it really is. The mind might have difficulty associating sleep with your bed if it interacts with it on a regular basis as part of your everyday living space. This has been shown to significantly worsen insomnia symptoms. In its place, remove your living space from your bedroom and begin to use other sections of your home for these everyday activities.

5. Before going to bed, do some mental activities to keep your mind from wandering. No,

I'm not suggesting that you use this as an excuse to spend time on your phone playing brain games. Obtain some pens, pencils, erasers, paper, and puzzle books from the local stationery shop. Alternatively, you might purchase a book from the bookstore that you are interested in reading. Get a magazine and spend some time reading the comics or doing the crossword puzzles. Activate your mind by playing a game of scrabble or a single-player card game and thinking about the topics you need to think about. Do some math or jot down some thoughts in a diary. Yes, throw out the technology and get back to basics. This not only serves to divert your attention away from overthinking, but it also aids in the production of melatonin, making it simpler for you to fall and remain asleep at night.

6. Become acquainted with relaxation techniques.

As a result, unless you are ready to create a CD full of soothing music, beta wave audio playlists, and guided meditation films, this should be the sole reason you utilize technology. While you are lying down to relax, you should breathe in through your nose and out through your mouth. Use your stomach and intestines to breathe rather than your chest. This helps you get more oxygen into your body while also waking up your brain, which makes it calm down and relax.

7. Super-thick blankets

The added comfort provided by heavy blankets is invaluable while traveling. When we snuggle with someone, we get a sense of warmth and intimacy. A thick blanket has the same effect as a hefty pillow. If you have no trouble falling asleep but wake up frequently throughout the night, the thick blanket acts as a safety net, allowing you to fall back asleep with little to no effort. The use of peaceful music in the background while sleeping is a terrific option if you suffer from maintenance insomnia. When you wake up, the music will help you fall back asleep since the music is so soothing to the ears.

Hopefully, these approaches will be of assistance, and you will be able to sleep well. However, if you keep using these strategies, particularly an hour or two before your bedtime, you will find that sleep will arrive sooner rather than later. In addition to these strategies, make sure that your "worry time" occurs well before you go to sleep. In the event that you spend too much time worrying and going through your thoughts close to when you intend to sleep, those worries and thoughts may carry over into your bedtime routine, making it more difficult to fall asleep because your brain will learn that when it's time to sleep, it's also time to think, which is counterproductive. That is something we do not desire.

TECHNIQUES FOR MAKING DECISIONS AND SOLVING PROBLEMS (DMT)

It is a proven truth that in order to tackle intricate or hard tasks, you must have good decision-making abilities. As a side note, it is also true that in order to be a successful problem solver, you must be aware that the choices you make determine the result of a solution. I've merged these two portions into a single one since they're like two peas in a pod, so to speak. Everything we learn about decision-making will be applied to the way you address challenges in the future. If you want more assistance with problem solving, the final chapter contains a number of highly helpful strategies on the subject. Every talent has a corresponding skill that must be learnt or that may be taught. The following abilities are required for good decision-making:

- Examining the various options available to us in order to achieve the desired result or outcome;
- a sense of self-awareness or introspection;
- Possibility of thinking creatively or analytically;
- Abilities in effective communication

- The ability to work as part of a team.

These abilities are required in order for us to be able to examine our own attitudes and ideas in order to make a choice and stick to it. When individuals make several choices that lead to our official destination, it is beneficial to be organized and creative in order to execute and choose them apart in order to get one step closer to the final decision.

The following abilities are required for good problem-solving abilities:

- Ability to think creatively as well as rationally
- The ability to conduct research
- Capabilities in effective communication and socialization
- ·Emotional intelligence is a skill that can be learned.

Making a decision is important.

Do you see a trend here? Almost all five of these abilities are interconnected in some way with the decision-making process. In order to improve at both of these talents, it is beneficial to build emotional intelligence, which helps you think for yourself, reflect on your views, and experience empathy for others. The development of emotional intelligence leads to the development of social intelligence, which is the ability to communicate effectively in order to get what you want or need in a courteous way.

So let's take a closer look at what the issue is. A problem is comprised of objectives and impediments. If we set ourselves goals to achieve, there are hills or mountains in our way, which are referred to as barriers that prevent us from achieving our objectives. Problem resolution is the process of removing these roadblocks in order to achieve our end destination, our objectives.

STAGES IN THE PROCESS OF SOLVING A PROBLEM

Prior to solving an issue, we must first go through all of the phases of the problem:

1. Determining the nature of the issue:

This is the point at which the issue manifests itself. At this level, the issue may seem to be dispersed and unclear, making it appear to be quite large. Nevertheless, if you think about and identify it, you will be able to describe what the actual problem is.

2. Investigating the nature of the issue

During this phase, we learn to notice and deconstruct the difficulties that arise as a result of the original problem. We examine the obstacles and conduct research on them. When we do this, we generate a clearer image in our brains of how we may solve the issue.

3. Identifying and compiling a list of possible solutions

After you have defined and broken down the issue, as well as identified and eliminated every obstacle, you may begin looking for potential solutions. You may create a list of possible outcomes depending on your ability to think outside the box while looking for a solution. Without going into too much detail, this is where our brains are actively engaged in trying to discover a solution.

4. Making a choice is number four.

Once we've compiled a list of potential answers, it's time to make a choice. We may utilize our logical thinking abilities or our communication skills to choose the best option in our previous stage, if we have them. Afterwards, once we've made a choice, we stick to it and continue our journey.

5. Taking the required actions

Here we are at the end of the process, when we have utilized all of our talents to come to a final conclusion, and we are putting that decision into action! We don't look back while we're moving ahead; if we make a mistake, we only learn from it later on in life. Taking action does not imply that we should second-guess our choice or that we should listen to the noise in our heads that tells us to turn back. What we must do now is overcome our fear that we have done all we can and accept that this is what we will do from here on out. Essentially, issue solving is the process of devising strategies for completing a tough or complex activity in order to accomplish our aim or destination. It is the decision-making process that determines how fast we are able to overcome the obstacles and find solutions to these challenges. The tendency of our thoughts to get in the way with excessive overthinking or second-guessing is why we must learn how to make judgments without second-guessing them afterwards.

How to Improve Your Decision-Making Capabilities

Through the course of this book, we have discussed how to turn off the mental chatter, how to reset the mind, and how to conquer our phobias. The reason most individuals struggle with their decision-making abilities is that they postpone putting the solution into action because they want to ensure that it is the right option that will not result in failure. Being a perfectionist leads to procrastination throughout the decision-making process, which is why failure is only implemented when you are afraid that you have not done your best. Stopping this cycle may be accomplished by believing in yourself that whatever choice you have made or are going to make has been completely explored and defined intellectually or physically, and that there is no other alternative. Make judgments with confidence, and if the results aren't what you anticipated, use the experience to improve your future selections. At the end of the day, the only result you should expect is positivity. Let's start with the fundamentals. After that, we'll go through several different ways of making these selections while still keeping the fundamentals in mind:

MAKE A SCHEDULE FOR SOME QUALITY THINKING TIME.

As long as you purposefully set aside some time in your day to think about the "issue" at hand, you will be able to figure out what your options are for dealing with it.

Make a list of your considerations.

In the same way that you define the issue, you must also identify and set out your options for solving it. Select a number of choices that are based on one issue at a time and go from there. When you have all of your options set out in front of you, you can take a step back and assess which path is the best one to follow.

Consider all of your options before making a decision.

Every option you have considered up to this point should have been thoroughly researched and considered. Make no more decisions because the more decisions you make, the more likely it is that you will end up with a larger slice of pie that you will be unable to eat. The alternatives you have today (which are restricted to three to five) are the ones that need to be carefully considered in order for you to solve your issue and achieve your objective in the shortest possible time. Now that the basics have been explained, here are some more things you can do that use the basics:

1. Examine your morals and values to see what they are.

This is significant because it increases our self-awareness and allows us to see the decision-making process in a manner that we will not want to turn away from. Consider the following scenario: For their sake, you are faced with two options: one might place your buddy in a position where you are not comfortable, and you would be sacrificing for their sake; the other option puts you on top and makes them your "sidekick." You must choose one of these alternatives depending on which one will provide you with the greatest level of happiness. If seeing your buddy in a better position than they are currently is important to you because you have other plans for yourself, then choice one is preferable to option two. If, on the other hand, your buddy is already in a strong position and you need to be the one on top, the second alternative is the preferable one. Make sure that you stay true to your core values, no matter what they are. Playing "what-if" games is never fun or beneficial.

2. Imagine what will happen as a result of your actions.

Close your eyes and visualize what you believe will happen as a result of the choices you have made. Consider the best-case and worst-case possibilities for the situation at hand. Give yourself a five-minute time restriction and don't try to ponder too hard. Once the timer runs off, choose the option that you were most satisfied with at the conclusion of the process.

3. Put it through its paces.

This comes into play in certain instances, but not all of them. For example, if your employment requires you to relocate, you should go to the city to which you will be relocating and assess your sentiments about the location. If it seems right, then go for it; if it feels wrong, then heed your instincts and don't go on with the project.

3. Pay attention to your hopes

Using your hopes as a compass, you can navigate through life using your gut sense. It's your intuition screaming at you to do something, and you should listen. So it's possible that your heart is in one place and your intellect is in another. What would you like to see on the other side of a coin if you were to flip one? If you were to ask someone for advice, what would you hope they would say in response? Whatever your instincts may be, pay attention to them. If you make a choice on the basis of disavowing these expectations, you may not be satisfied with the consequences in the end and may spend endless hours wishing you had chosen the other option instead. Listen to your instincts; most of the time, they are correct.

YOU SHOULD HAVE SELF-ASSURANCE WHILE SETTING AND ACHIEVING YOUR GOALS.

In other words, self-confidence is the feeling of being positively confident that you are accurate in your judgments, talents, power, values, and choices, to name a few things. While it is similar to self-esteem in that it is an appraisal of one's own value, self-confidence is the capacity to completely trust in one's own ability to do everything one sets their minds to. Self-esteem is an evaluation of one's own worth. Some traits of a person who is self-assured are as follows:

- They do what they believe to be right, regardless of whether others agree or condemn them;
- They are adamant about obtaining what they desire and will go to any length to obtain it;
- This means they acknowledge their errors and accept responsibility for their conduct.
- They are patient in waiting for acceptance or approval because they do not believe they are worthy of recognition or acknowledgment.
- It is not in their nature to extol or brag about their successes.

- They are gracious in accepting accolades.
- The fact that they are comfortable with being vulnerable.
- They are not tempted to exert control or be envious of others.
- They will not accept responsibility if a relationship fails, and they will not blame the other person.
- They are self-assured in their ability to make sound decisions; and
- They are self-aware and forceful in their behavior.

All of these attributes are ideal for setting and achieving objectives as well as realizing one's own personal potential. Being self-assured implies that you are willing to take chances and have minimal fear of the unknown since you are secure in your ability to complete the tasks at hand.

INCREASING ONE'S SELF-CONFIDENCE

In the event that these attributes do not sound like you, be assured that they may be acquired with practice. Developing or working on your confidence is not mandatory. Yet, if you do not do so, you will still be able to get what you want. However, it will take longer and your objectives may be farther away than you would like. In order to achieve your intended objective, it may seem as if you are climbing a never-ending mountain of difficulties. Some people refer to this as "the way of life," but is this really the only way to live? Below you will find some suggestions on how to grow or boost your confidence levels.

1. The First Step Is Creating Your Adventure Plan

While preparing yourself for self-confidence, you should pay attention to the following five factors: These are detailed in further detail below. To begin your voyage, you must first determine where you are now located, where you want to go, and whether or not you believe in yourself that you can and will accomplish your goals. You must cultivate a positive attitude and be open to this kind of dedication to transformation. Take a look back at your accomplishments. When you think about your accomplishments, try to think of at least five things that you have done well in your life so far. Did you ever come in first place in a marathon? Did you take first place in a hot dog eating contest? Were you an honors student in high school who had straight A's? Did you ever assist a cat in descending from a tree? Or do you want to save a life? Whatever your accomplishments are, no matter how large or small, they all matter.

Take note of your assets.

Once you've created your success list, you may use it to determine your own personal characteristics. Perhaps you didn't perform to your full potential in one of these accomplishments, and you want to learn how to perform better or more effectively in the future. Once you've identified your own personal strengths, you may go on to identify your own personal objectives and the obstacles that stand in the way of achieving those goals. Consider what you want to accomplish with your life. What do you want to be doing? And who do you hope to be in the future? It is never too late to embark on this journey of discovery.

Decide what is most essential to you and prioritize your goals accordingly.

Setting and achieving objectives is the most important factor in boosting your self-esteem and self-confidence. Self-confidence is mostly based on your capacity to fulfill and work towards your objectives, as well as your ability to continue to set new ones. The greater your degree of accomplishment, the greater your sense of self-worth will be. Whatever happens, confidence is about learning to grow from your errors and striving even harder the next time you face a similar situation. When you figure out what's most important to you, you'll discover that doing what you love isn't all that terrifying, and that making mistakes is just a normal part of the learning experience.

Maintain control of your thoughts.

This book is all about how to manage your thoughts. You must have a positive attitude throughout the whole procedure. Negative ideas should be challenged, and you should continue to reset your brain in order to get rid of those annoying anxieties. Work to overcome your negative side and embrace what you are good at. You will become more confident.

Make a commitment to success.

Taking the last step before embarking on your journey is possibly the most important: You must make a pledge to yourself that no matter what happens, you will remain committed to attaining your objectives through thick and thin. By doing so, you are effectively making a promise to yourself to take little steps forward every day in order to concentrate on your positivity, overcome those negative ideas, and become the greatest version of yourself. But wait, there's more to it than that; it believes in your ability to succeed, and it knows you will.

2. You should begin your journey.

This is the stage from which you go on your journey to finish your masterpiece. The self-awarded measure of all you have done should have been accomplished at this time. You should understand that your flaws will endure, but you should be proud of yourself for believing in yourself today. Because you respect and appreciate yourself, you should be able to state confidently and with pride that your commitment to becoming more is a result of this value and appreciation. Begin with modest, manageable victories and build your way up by fulfilling greater and bigger objectives as you proceed. Take pride in your accomplishments and lavish yourself with lavish rewards for each one. This is one of the most effective ways to improve self-confidence more quickly.

Increase your knowledge.

Take a look at your list of objectives once you have completed it. Examine your list of strengths and determine which abilities you will need to acquire or master in order to achieve the objectives you have set for yourself. Once you have a clear understanding of how to achieve your objectives, enroll in a course and get information about the procedures necessary to attain them. Make an effort to get certificates and become certified for the tasks you want to do.

Concentrate on the fundamentals.

Do tiny things well, and you'll go a long way. Don't strive for perfection; instead, make changes and concentrate on the fundamentals. Especially when you are just starting out, you don't want to overload yourself with complicated or creative ambitions that are just beyond the reach of your current abilities. This will be addressed later.

Make little objectives for yourself and see them through to completion.

In the beginning, stick to this routine: set a goal, achieve it, celebrate your accomplishment, and then move on to something a bit more challenging than the last objective you achieved. The purpose of this phase is to establish a pattern of making and achieving goals in your life. Your objectives will only grow in size over time, but the secret is to do it in such a steady manner that, by the time you reach the farthest goal you have been working for, you will not have noticed the rising difference in difficulty.

Continue to focus on your mental faculties.

Continue to remain on top of fighting those negative ideas and over-thinking chatter that are running through your head. Continue to go forward with optimism and let go of whatever anxieties you may have about the future.

3. The third step is to strive forward toward success and to act.

This is the point at which you take action to accomplish every step that has come before it. This is the step that will lay the groundwork for all of your future triumphs. You have finished figuring out your journey here, you have accomplished your trip quest, and you are now ready to put all of the information you have gathered to use. This is the point at which you take action in order to complete more difficult and time-consuming objectives. With each objective achieved, you get more benefits and a greater sense of accomplishment. When you have achieved your desired goal—for example, owning a large piece of real estate and serving as a manager for a large corporation—you can take pride in all of your previous accomplishments and be confident in your ability to succeed in anything else you undertake because you have been doing it the entire time. Self-confidence is not something that develops overnight, but rather something that, after a few years (or even weeks or months), you will be able to state that you are more confident now than you were the day you began this journey.

Changing Your Interpersonal Relationships with Others

Many times, the individuals we surround ourselves with are the sources of our inner negativity, and we have little control over it. Overthinking is impacted by our choices as much as what we are told by our employer. It is time for us to make decisions for ourselves now that we have learnt how to be more confident in making these better-informed judgments in the first place.

Some pointers on how to recognize a negative person in your life are included below:

They are a source of concern.

They have strong feelings about your life; they are judgmental.

- They keep their identities secret.
- They have a pessimistic view of the world;
- Their reactions to your proposals and everything you tell them are sensitive.
- They are the complaint kings and queens.
- They prefer the word "but";
- They make no significant effort to better themselves or their lives.
- They invent excuses not to do anything.
- They sap all of your energy; and
- They notice the flaws in everything that is wonderful;
- They are self-centered.

How to Deal with a Negative Individual

It is possible that your happiness is influenced by the connections you have and the company you maintain. As a result of interacting with negative individuals, your good vibes may begin to dwindle, and you may find yourself falling back into the same bad behaviors that you were engaged in before you picked up this book. It makes sense that so many of us are sponges for other people's behavior since we are social beings. While we make every effort not to offend those we care about, there are moments when we are confused about whether or not we have done anything wrong to upset them. Of course, not everyone can get along, but we make every effort to do so. Dealing with a negative person may be really challenging, but here is the most important thing to remember while dealing with them: You have no control over them; all you have power over is how you react as a consequence of being in their presence. If you believe that establishing boundaries and being forceful will allow you to repair, heal, or continue your relationship with this individual, go ahead. If you are unable to do so and every encounter with them appears to bring you down despite your best attempts, it is advisable to either get rid of them completely or reduce the amount of time you spend with them. Some helpful strategies for coping with poor or poisonous relationships are as follows:

- Set healthy boundaries.

Negative individuals are unable to recognize when they are being negative, much less take into account the sentiments of others as a consequence of their negativity. When you are engaging with a toxic individual, it is important to consider both internal and external boundaries. Make a promise to yourself that you will not allow them to make you feel horrible about yourself. If your mood or thoughts begin to shift while you are in the presence of this individual, you must leave immediately. Kindly tell them that if they can't learn how to be more positive, you won't join in on the conversation. Then, respectfully, walk away from them.

Another step you might take is to initiate the conversation. Before you discuss anything with them, get them hyped up and make them feel good about themselves. While telling a negative person to be positive makes them feel criticized, if you behave positively and make them experience positivity, your vibe may help them feel lighter, and they will reciprocate that positivity throughout the conversation. This may result in a stronger sense of community and fewer conflicts.

- Call the worth of this friendship or romantic relationship into question.

Several questions concerning your interpersonal connections should be asked of yourself before the end of this article. Try making a list of all the individuals you know about whom you wish to learn more. Ask yourself: "Who exactly is this person in my eyes? What is the nature of my connection with them? Are they a detrimental influence? "How often do you simply hang out because you want to, or do you hang out because they require something from you? " The answers to these questions may come as a surprise to some, while others may not. On the other hand, the responses will assist you in determining if the connection is worth maintaining or whether it may be better to just you should consider their motivations for offering advice, as well as your own feelings about the dialogue as you go forward. Is it because they really care about your needs that they advise you to do something, or is it because they have an opinion on what you should or shouldn't do that they urge you to do something? Those that are optimistic are less concerned with what others think of them because they are secure in their ability to accomplish what is good for them. Make a point of paying closer attention to the words they are using so that you can understand what they are trying to convey. Walk away from them totally.

Don't take things personally, even if they seem to be personal.

It is possible that everything a negative person says to you is because they are having a terrible day, because they have their own beliefs, because they are judge mental, or because they believe they are attempting to assist you by offering you advice. However,

- Rather than reacting, take action.

Individuals who struggle with optimism are likely to stand out to us when we look at our list, which we produced. Knowing this, the next time you come face to-face with this person, deliberately produce pleasant sentiments in your mind and don't wait for a chance to do so. Informing them of anything you appreciate about them might help to lift their spirits and give them a boost. This may provide them with some respite and set the stage for what they may anticipate from you in the future.

- Determine whether the connection is genuine or not.

Most of the time, we observe things in our own way and then attempt to persuade others to see things our way as well. We may express surprise when someone does not heed our counsel, which might cause us to get enraged or uneasy. When dealing with a negative individual, consider the reality of your connection as well as the reality of the other person. What is it about them that is so negative? What can you do to assist them in remaining optimistic while maintaining your own sanity? This implies that after you have completed all of your tasks, you may relax. Take these negative individuals in little doses and you will see a shift in your perception of the reality of the relationship. Starting with the statement, "All I can do for my buddy is love them for who they are," begins to build your confidence. I will assist them when they need it, but if they are unable to accept change, I must do what is best for me while still being considerate of their requirements.

- You do not have problem-solving skills.

According to a popular adage, "you cannot assist someone who does not want to be helped." 1. Instead of spending your time and energy trying to assist a negative person who is unwilling to change, you may have to accept that they are in this situation. It is necessary to let go of what you cannot control in order to overcome excessive anxiety. So, when your bad company continues to be negative, remind yourself that you are not their buddy, and that you are not there to fix their issues for them. You have earned their friendship by making the decision to be there for them. If there comes a point in your life when you have no choice but to walk away, here is what you may need to do. Don't feel bad about yourself.

Your Relationship with Your Spouse Can Be Improved.

A toxic spouse, in addition to poisonous negativity in the company you keep, might be even more detrimental to your negative thought-patterns than a toxic company. Relationships are difficult, and they require effort on both sides. However, a relationship is not always poisonous because both partners are sick; sometimes it is just one of you who is unhealthy. A toxic person—or spouse—might be completely unaware that they are toxic or that they are negatively affecting you. Here are a few things to ask yourself in order to determine whether or not you are in a toxic relationship: ·How do you feel when you are in the company of this individual?

- ·Do you feel comfortable when you are in the presence of this individual?
- How has your marriage affected your children and your life?
- While spending time with them, do you get emotional tension or exhaustion from the situation?

- Do you find yourself becoming more uptight when you are around them? Is this individual manipulative or deceptive in any way?
- ·How do you feel when you are with them, as opposed to when you are not with them?
- Do you find that life is more difficult than it needs to be while you are together?
- If you're like most people, you find yourself altering your lifestyle to meet the wants of your partner.

These responses may significantly challenge your assumptions and assist you in determining what you should do next. The majority of individuals remain in relationships because they get some benefit from their partner's company. Among them are things such as feelings of warmth and closeness; money; power; children; what you have established together; love; and the incapacity to see unfavorable developments. Most of the time, we remain because we get caught up in the idea that things will change or that if we do this, then that will happen. Even if we have a good reason to stay, we need to think about whether it is in our best interests to stay or leave the situation.

MAKING A POSITIVE DIFFERENCE IN YOUR RELATIONSHIP

If you have decided to give it another go, there are a few things you should consider doing that you may not have done before. If none of the options on the following list work out for you, professional counseling may be a better option in your situation. However, because it takes two to restore a relationship to health, you must assess how much energy you should devote to your efforts. You and your partner must make a commitment to getting to know one another again (since people change over time) and to investing more time in developing discipline, compromise, drive, and desire in your relationship. If these characteristics have been lost, there are methods for regaining them via the use of positive thinking. Each day, make a commitment to accomplish something together that will help to rebuild respect and love in your relationship. Some suggestions to assist you get back on track or "alter" your current relationship are as follows:

1. Talk to your partner about your concerns.

Staying on track requires communicating clearly with your spouse about what you need and what the issue is, and then working together to resolve these concerns. When you have been with someone for a long period of time, you begin to get familiar with their habits, their routine, and their manner of living. We, on the other hand, neglect to communicate our worries, which frequently results in arguments or conflicts amongst people. Use a low tone and a calm voice while you're speaking to avoid sounding agitated. Try not to be a nag about your concerns, and instead have a positive attitude throughout.

2. Use "I" statements to communicate with others.

"You" remarks, such as "you aren't doing enough" or "you forced me to do these things as revenge," are often used in our conversations. Something that should be made crystal clear is that your spouse will never be held accountable for your ideas or behaviors. You are responsible for your own decisions, and "you" utterances might come off as blaming or bullying. If you want to prevent this antagonism, try using "I" statements, such as "I feel wounded because..." or "I am disturbed because..." When you tell your spouse how they are making you feel, you should also tell them what they can do to make you feel better in the same phrase. To offer an example, "I feel insulted when you don't call me while you're out; next time, I'd appreciate it if you could give me a call and return my calls."

3. Maintain a high level of consistency.

It is necessary to discuss problems and then come up with remedies for them. Stick to your new "rules" and limits that you have established for your relationship once you have established clear ones. Remind your spouse of these dialogues if they have insulted you, and ask them to remind you of the same if you have fallen off the wagon. It takes a team effort to change your relationship, and it will take time for your partnership to become healthy again.

4. Always be true to yourself and the best version of yourself.

If you are not in control of your own desires, needs, and emotions, you will be unable to concentrate on a relationship and the rigorous requirements it places on you. So, as you practice all of the tactics in this book, be sure to include them in every interaction you have in order to become a happier and healthier version of yourself. When it comes to individuals you care about, never settle for anything less than what you know you are capable of.

5. Invest in some much-needed quality time together.

When it comes to relationships, they are about much more than simply arguing and getting to know one another better as time goes by. Yes, you will argue and have disputes, but the more time you spend together in a non-argumentative manner, the stronger your relationship will develop, even though the most difficult moments. Quality time is about putting aside distractions like your phone and engaging in one-on-one conversation with your partner. Play a card game, relax in front of the fireplace, or take a walk in the evening. Rekindle your romance by doing activities you've been wanting to do and reminiscing about the events that led up to your initial meeting.

6. The sense of touch is vital.

In addition to spending quality time together, touch is also important. Physical contact has been shown in several studies to be effective in releasing the endorphins that are required to make you joyful. Introduce contact into your relationship by holding their hand in public or stroking their shoulder or back as you pass by. The next stage is to curl up on the sofa with a book (without intercourse). The importance of physical contact in a relationship, even when there is no sexual interaction, speaks volumes about the quality of the connection. When the opportunity presents itself, go one step farther and make the caressing more sexual.

7. Recognize the importance of communication.

Everything we do is based on communication with one another. Arguments make us feel bad about ourselves; laughter makes us feel better about ourselves. Positive or negative feelings at the conclusion of a discussion are influenced by how we speak, listen to, and react throughout our talks. The sound of quiet may convey a great deal when words aren't enough to express your feelings. Pick up some communication books or consult with a specialist to discover effective methods to communicate with your spouse and vice versa.

8. Stay faithful to your own personal ideals and principles throughout this process.

No matter whom you are or what you do, no one should ever put you in a position where you have to second guess your priorities. Make a list of the items that are unassailable and will not be negotiable, followed by a list of the things that are "maybes." Make a list of your key principles and make sure your spouse is aware of the fact that they are crucially limited in their ability to maintain them. When someone is uncompromising, here is how you can remain loyal to yourself and choose whether or not to move away from them.

9. Pay attention to your companion.

When taking communication lessons, one of the first things you will learn is that listening is half the fight. When you're listening to your partner's needs and desires, give your whole attention to what they're saying. This includes turning off all distractions, such as music, television, and outside sounds, among other things. Take care to meet at a place that is both peaceful and out of the way, especially if you are in the midst of a hectic day. You will be able to hear and attempt to grasp what your companion is saying in this manner. In order to communicate effectively, it is essential to first listen carefully before speaking.

10. Be clear about your desires.

As soon as you've recognized the areas in which your relationship has failed (or is on the verge of failing), it's critical that you convey what you want to your partner. Inquire as to what they would want to see, and then tell them what you would like to see happen more often in the future. Because no one can read the thoughts of another, articulating your desires to your partner may significantly strengthen your relationship. Perhaps they have been holding something back for a long time, and if you are willing to listen to what they have to say without passing judgment, you will be able to learn how to collaborate more effectively.

STEP SEVEN: IMPLEMENT SIMPLE DAILY PRACTICES TO GET RID OF PROCRASTINATION

Everybody can relate to procrastination since there isn't anybody who would argue with the fact that it exists. Procrastination will have played a part in your life at least once or twice, if not more than that. When you miss your deadlines, the amount of tension increases over your head, and you are compelled to finish the assignment as quickly as possible to avoid further consequences. However, you are well aware that it will be difficult to accomplish due to the overwhelming amount of work. Regardless, you make an attempt! Procrastination will make your life a living hell. Therefore, avoid making it a habit as much as possible.

There are some individuals who wish to stop procrastinating, but they are unable to do so because they do not understand how to do so. Alternatively, they may be lacking the necessary motivation at times. I understand that it might be frustrating. In order to comprehend the reality that procrastination variables vary from one person to another, you must first grasp what they are.

A writer will put off working on the assignment to which he or she has been assigned. After that, he or she will have to labor around the clock to finish the assignment.

A student will put off schoolwork until the last minute, only to do it at the last minute.

People who play sports are going to forget to take their medicine because they are so focused on the game right now.

By evaluating each of the examples above, you will come to the conclusion that procrastination will have an impact on each and every person stated in the case. For example, if an athlete does not seek treatment for an injury immediately, he or she will be forced to cope with a slew of serious problems. In the same way, there will be a great number of emotional consequences as well.

I'm going to discuss with you some of the practical everyday techniques that you may use to help you overcome procrastination. When you follow these steps, you will be able to overcome procrastination even when you are feeling sluggish or uninspired. Before you begin reading about the techniques listed below, keep in mind that you are free to choose any of them that interest you. This implies that you are not obligated to engage in all of the behaviors listed here. Let's get this party started!

1. Identify potential crises and devise solutions to them.

While procrastination is a poor habit in and of itself, it is also a potentially deadly one. It will have a significant influence on your overall health. Occasionally, you may even lose sight of the strong relationships that you formerly enjoyed with your family members. They may even come to believe that you no longer care about what they think. There may be times in your life when you will have to deal with unforeseen priorities such as death, illness, and a variety of other things. Such issues cannot be postponed since you will be required to deal with them immediately. In such a case, you would be required to cancel all of the previously planned tasks. Other times, wonderful family gatherings might devolve into awful circumstances, and you are powerless to prevent them from occurring and returning to your job. Because emergencies don't give you a heads-up, you'll have to deal with the difficulties they bring with them. What steps can you take to avert an emergency? Are you going to put everything on hold and deal with the problem? Alternatively, if you have previously postponed the task and then something important comes up, how do you intend to deal with the situation? What may happen if you choose to disregard an emergency?

To effectively deal with crises, you must first have a clear understanding of the types of situations you are dealing with. You may want to consider the ramifications of avoiding the emergency situation. Another option is to consider the individuals who are involved in the situation. How will they feel if you choose to disregard it? What steps could you take to resolve this unexpected problem and return to your previous job? If the emergency isn't life-threatening, can you put it off until later?

Permit me to share some information with you before you continue. If you are working so hard that you don't even have time for your family, it indicates that you are missing out on a lot of the wonderful things in life and that there is a lack of balance in your life, as described above. When you are not working, you are not living your life – and here is where the notion of smart working comes into play. It is quite easy to get preoccupied and lose sight of the people around you. Alternatively, you might easily put off crises that you perceive are not serious, and such emergencies may develop into life-threatening circumstances as a result. Of course, you could be so busy that you don't even have time for the most essential things, but it all comes down to your priorities in life.

There is no project, appointment, or meeting that can be put on hold for the sake of an emergency that might end up affecting the life of a loved one. When something crucial comes up, I'd recommend putting other things on hold since procrastination affects not just business but also personal relationships. If you deal with crises as soon as they arise, you will avoid having to deal with the worst instances later on.

Most of the time, we believe that procrastination is all about work and how we postpone our job performance. However, I hope I have brought your attention to something that you should also consider.

In the event that you plan and execute work-related tasks before the deadline, or if you have done half of the job before the deadline, unanticipated priorities may not have a significant influence on your work life. Organization and knowing how to put your life in order are important parts of living a happy life.

2. Conduct daily assessments of the situation

Another effective method of avoiding procrastination is to do daily evaluations of your work. Investing only 10 minutes each day will allow you to keep track of how things are progressing. When you are reviewing your day, you will be able to identify the most important tasks to do. After that, you may look at the tasks that will have a significant influence on your short-term objectives. Consider using a Q&A structure for this review session in order to make it more straightforward. What are the next meetings that you will be required to attend? Are there any emails that you need to respond to today? If so, please list them here. Currently, are there any papers that need to be revised? Is there anything on your schedule that will take up more time than you have allotted? What are the tasks that need more concentration?

In the same way, you should participate in a Q&A session to learn about the day's schedule. However, you are not required to limit yourself to the questions I have provided. Instead, you may prepare your own Q & A and then follow along with the others. If you do this daily assessment, you will be able to comprehend the overall structure of the day. The ability to remain on track will be greatly enhanced after you have completed your plan. You will be well-versed in the duties that need more time or a rapid reaction. It means that as a result, you will not procrastinate because you know that it will hurt your goals.

If you want to discover one of the most effective techniques for overcoming procrastination, it is known as the Pareto Principle. It's all about the 80/20 rule in this situation. Make an effort to learn more about this idea before you try to use it in your daily life.

3. MITS, which stands for "Most Important Tasks,"

If you start your day with a to-do list that is overflowing with obligations, it will be difficult to overcome procrastination. If you want to get things done on time and properly, you must simplify your to-do list as much as possible. What steps can you take to make your to-do list more manageable? If you concentrate on MIT's most critical job, it is rather straightforward. To succeed, you must accept assignments that will have a significant impact on your long-term goals. Many productivity gurus, including those who specialize in time management, encourage doing so.

My recommendation is to prioritize the top three most critical chores that must be completed before the end of the day. It is preferable to choose two significant activities with tight deadlines, as well as one activity that will have an influence on your long-term professional aim. MIT's idea will help you avoid procrastination if you keep an eye on it at all times. Once you have completed the two most essential tasks of the day, you will be more interested in participating in the remaining activities by the evening. And that kind of drive is essential if you want to be successful in your battle against procrastination.

4. The Eisenhower Matrix (also known as the Eisenhower Matrix).

Who doesn't like being productive? It's hard not to be relieved when things go exactly as planned. However, things don't always turn out the way you want them to. If your life is anything like mine, it is packed with frequent crises and changes, and you must be able to make rapid judgments in order to survive.

If you want to make a speedy choice, you'll need the help of the Eisenhower Matrix to get you there. Dwight Davis Eisenhower, the man who came up with the idea, was a general in the army at the time. It was for this reason that he came up with the notion. Being in the army makes it difficult to constantly carry out the plan exactly as it is laid out. There will be drastic and significant changes in the future. It was the Eisenhower Matrix idea that served as guidance in such a situation.

If Eisenhower was able to use this strategy in the army, there is no reason why we cannot use it in our personal lives to prevent procrastinating as well! When dealing with this notion, it's important not to lose sight of the four quadrants that surround it. By concentrating on the four quadrants, you will be able to approach your daily duties in the most appropriate manner. Permit me to describe the four quadrants in further detail:

Quadrant 1: This is extremely urgent as well as critical.

As a result, they are the chores that must be accomplished first since they are much more significant than any other duties and because they are directly related to your professional objectives. Furthermore, you must finish the duties as soon as possible since they are time-sensitive. Complete these duties successfully and you will be able to prevent unfavorable effects in the future. Once you have accomplished your Q1 objectives, you will be ready to turn your attention to other projects. In the case of a project that must be done and turned in by a certain time of the day, you should give it your full attention because it is both important and urgent.

Quadrant 2 consists of the following: Although necessary, it is not urgent.

Despite the fact that the tasks in Q2 are significant, they are not urgent. Despite the fact that they may have a significant influence, they are not as time-sensitive as Q1. When you compare Q2 to Q1, you will be able to plainly see the difference between the two. Most of the time, Q2 assignments will include those that have a significant influence on your long-term career or life objectives. Yes, you will need to devote more time and attention to these responsibilities. However, you seldom execute it because your subconscious understands that the chores in Q2 can wait. In the meantime, you'll be concentrating on the duties in the other quadrants. Make sure you don't make this mistake since your long-term objectives are the driving force behind your short-term ambitions. For example, your health is one of the most crucial things, and if you do not devote sufficient attention to it, you will come to regret it. However, if you get overburdened, it is doubtful that you will have time to complete Q2 activities. In particular, you do not need to respond to anybody about your Q2 responsibilities.

Quadrant 3: "Despite being urgent, it is not essential.

Although the activities listed under Q3 are urgent, you do not have to devote all of your time to them. You have two options: automate duties or assign them to someone who is capable of doing the job. Because these jobs are not very vital, it is acceptable to assign them. These responsibilities are often assigned by a third party, and the tasks listed under Q3 will have no direct impact on your career objectives. However, while you are managing Q3 duties, you must make a record of the work that you assign to other people. In the case of a phone call while working on a time-sensitive assignment, you may get sidetracked by picking up the phone and answering it. Alternatively, it may not even be a critical decision in certain cases. You may appoint someone to carry out such tasks. Even if the call is urgent, you may still allocate it to a person who will be able to handle it effectively. The ability to control your day will result as a result of this.

Quadrant 4 (or the fourth quadrant):

Not important in addition to not urgent.

The jobs listed under Q4 are those that should be avoided at all costs. These duties eat up valuable time that might be spent elsewhere. Spending no time on Q4 chores will allow you to devote more time to the things falling under Q2 responsibilities. You should have a good idea of what the Q4 tasks are. However, they include activities like watching television, browsing the internet, playing video games, and a variety of other things. So, do you think you should get rid of Q4? No, not at all! You shouldn't do it. If you don't maintain a healthy balance in your life, you may find it difficult to keep your employment. The tasks in Q4 will assist you anytime you need to take a 5-minute break or whenever you need to take a break from your workday to relax. During a time when you are attempting to be productive, these duties should not even be on your radar.

Make a table on a sheet of paper or a page in your diary to get an idea of how to implement the Eisenhower Matrix in your life. Separate the table into four columns and seven rows by using a ruler. Divide the rows according to the days of the week, and then add the quadrants to the columns according to the days of the week. When your table is ready, sit down and think about your week. However, you should not write anything down just yet. Before you begin your day, take some time to reflect, examine it again, and assign the duties according to the matrix. When something new comes up, you need to think about what kind of assignment it is and then put it in the right quadrant.

The table may be studied after you have completed all seven days in order to determine your efficacy and production. When you do this for the first time, it will not be spectacular, but persevere and see it through. Continue to try, and you will soon find that you spend more time on the most important and urgent things.

Keep using this strategy and you will be able to arrange your day-to-day duties, which will allow you to achieve more and greater success.

5. 5. Complete the task as swiftly as possible.

Sometimes you come across chores that don't need much time, maybe even less than five minutes, yet you put them off. To give you an example, you could tidy up after supper, write an email, or even change into your pajamas (this is laziness). Despite the fact that these duties do not require much time, you do not do them because you perceive yourself to be overburdened.

By convincing yourself that you have too much on your plate, you may get away with disregarding fast or small duties. However, the issue is that every time you put off little activities, they pile up, and you may wind up having to deal with large projects at the end of the day. If you don't take action right now, you'll have a lot to accomplish when you finally get some time off. Another advantage of doing little activities quickly is that it prevents them from piling up and becoming larger duties later in the day. In order to do small jobs efficiently, you should examine the following two strategies: 1.

It is essential for you to adhere to the Two-Minute Rule, which is one of the techniques that you must use. Isn't it true that if you estimate that the work will take no more than two minutes or less, you should do it instead of putting it off?

When you come across a tiny activity, consider if it will take you longer to do it than you anticipated. Why not complete them if they aren't already? Additionally, if you maintain this behavior throughout your life, you will feel as if you are eliminating a great deal of negativity and will have more time to devote to vital things. Furthermore, you will have the impression that you are more organized and you will have accomplished more than you had before. In contrast, if you discover things that will take longer than five minutes to do, you must set aside time to complete them.

The second exercise is to complete all of the chores that are doable in a single sitting. Let me give you an example: you've gotten an email and, despite the fact that it demands a response, you put off responding to it until later. If you check it later, you will have forgotten the specifics contained inside the email itself, and you will be forced to go through the same process all over again. Instead of transforming a simple chore into a major headache, you may do it quickly and effortlessly. The principle of single handling aids you in completing the duties at your disposal.

If you can plainly see the end in front of you, you must take the required steps to get there. For example, you can wash the dishes straight immediately rather than putting them off until later in the day. Additionally, there are other brief chores that must be completed correctly once, such as typing. If you adhere to these principles, you will be able to perform little activities more quickly and effectively overcome procrastination issues. As a result of this method, it is possible to entirely remove the tension that comes with procrastination.

These are easy techniques that can assist you in overcoming procrastination. You do not need to be concerned or to feel horrible about yourself just because you are a procrastinator. Procrastination is something that everyone has done at some point in their life. Everyone has the ability to overcome procrastination if they put up the effort. You now have a plethora of practical suggestions that you may use. You can experiment with them to see if there are any differences!

You are much more powerful than you realize, and it is only you who has the ability to choose whether to become a procrastinator or a productive person.

TROUBLESHOOTING GUIDE (IN THE EVENT THAT NOTHING ELSE WORKS)

Aside from the end, this is a brief chapter in which we recap and put into practice everything we have learnt throughout this book. When you go off track and need some support on those dark and tough days, this chapter will serve as a quick guide to get you back on track.

GET YOUR LIFE BACK ON TRACK

Let's imagine you've done everything and put the strategies in this book to use, and then everything appears to be coming apart all of a sudden. In three simple steps, you can get back on track with your negative thought patterns, stop worrying about the little things, and stop overthinking everything. To get back on track, follow these three simple actions:

1. Determine the nature of the issue and its primary cause.

The majority of the time, when we attempt to do something new, our old habits try to seep back into our lives, making it that much more difficult to maintain our new routines. This is due to the fact that we have not identified the source of our issue. By addressing your triggers, you might attempt to re-identify the source of the issue. Here are some instances of triggers that may be prompting you to stray from your course:

- Anxiety caused by relationship changes;
- Boredom as a result of a lack of development;
- a chronic disease or injury that does not heal;
- A change in surroundings, such as relocating or taking a vacation;
- Trying to do too much too soon

Take some "me time" to find out what it was that caused you to fail in the first place in order to prevent your old patterns from creeping back into your life. Instead of seeing this as a setback, consider it an opportunity to start again with better information.

2. Restart the behavior by implementing your positive habit training.

Bring yourself back to the fundamentals and remind yourself that overthinking will only serve to make you less productive. Don't disregard your ideas; instead, notice them and cultivate awareness that they are even there in your head. Create a worry timetable and jot down your concerns to deal with them throughout this period of worry and anxiety. Practice meditation, and if you haven't been doing so lately, make a commitment to some physical activity. The slowness with which you perform these actions will push your brain to recall the habits you were attempting to establish and return you to the path of testing your mental patterns. When you get this down pat again, go back to the drawing board and set tiny objectives for yourself, rewarding yourself when you achieve them.

3. Play around with a new technique.

Not all means of action are effective for everyone, so experiment with several approaches to see which one works best for you. Suppose your concern time is just after dinner, around 6 p.m., and you start your worry time before dinner, at about 3 p.m. Alternatively, you may have gotten out of bed, begun working out, and then bathed, but you have failed since you are rushing through your day as a result of your pattern. Working out just before bed can help you sleep better. It's possible that by trying a new method, you'll come across something that works best for your timetable and getting back on track will be a breeze.

Anxiety (worrying) can be calmed in five minutes or less.

The presence of anxiety and other mood problems is widespread, and they might make it easier for old patterns to resurface. This is due to the fact that our concerns enable us to stick to what we know and feel "secure." It seems as if you are continuously having to restart because you give into your concerns and fall back rather than shooting ahead. Anxiety does not like change, and it will appear as though you are continually having to restart. The key to conquering this is to figure out effective methods of calming down instantly. Here are some suggestions about how to go about it:

1. Take part in the 5-5-5 game.

The 5-5-5 game is a strategy for gaining stability. Take a look around the room and list five items that you see. Close your eyes and take a deep breath in, then list five things you can hear in your head. Try to keep your eyes closed, or re-open them, and move five different body parts while naming each one. By moving your wrists and saying "wrist" aloud, you may make other such movements as well. Start again and repeat this process as many times as necessary until you feel peaceful. Imagine that everything is new to you and that you are experiencing it for the very first time, so you can fully enjoy the present moment.

2. Engage in a quick physical activity

Getting your body moving may include anything from jumping up and down to spinning in circles and stretching to using the muscles in your face to jiggle every part of your body to dancing. Exercise in whatever way you can, whether it's a quick jog or a fast stroll to get some fresh air or change your surroundings. Sometimes all your body needs is a little physical activity to get through the first adrenaline spike associated with worry. Keep an eye out for any weak sensations in your legs or tingling in your fingers when you're working out. Move through this, and you will be training your brain to deal with these unpleasant sensations in a healthy manner.

3. Apply a cool cloth to the back of your neck.

A cool rag around your neck, an ice cube in your hand, or a cold shower may all help to shock your nervous system and relieve stress. It is possible that all your body needs is a brief jolt to divert its focus away from anxiousness or worrying thoughts.

4. Squeeze a lemon or eat a banana.

Shocking your taste buds may also be a simple and effective way to shock your system. A lemon will cause your face to scrunch and your body to jolt, forcing the anxieties or overthinking that is generating the anxiety to end almost immediately. Bananas provide a plethora of nutrients that will help to restore your blood sugar levels back to normal. You may be having a sugar attack because you ate too much or not enough sugar. A banana can help you get your sugar levels back to normal, making you feel more relaxed.

5. Examine your anxious feelings.

Before you panic, take a moment to confront your ideas and feelings. Inquire about them. What exactly is the source of the anxiety? Which of the cognitive distortions do these ideas belong to and how do you know? Are you underestimating your ability to deal with this situation at the moment? Is it possible that this is a false alarm? What can you do to make a difference? What's the worst that can happen in this situation? When you take the time to fully answer these questions, you will discover that your mind does not have the attention span necessary to simultaneously transmit unpleasant sensations to your body and think about how to answer these questions. This may help you feel more relaxed. When you've finished answering these questions, take a moment to concentrate on your breathing, sit down, and be careful of your breaths.

METHODS FOR REDUCING NEGATIVE THINKING IN A SHORT AMOUNT OF TIME

On those days when your thought patterns have drowned out all the good, you may find yourself getting into a state of mindless chatter surrounded by negative thinking. To break out of this state of mind fast, use these simple steps.

1. **Cut it off at the knees.**

This approach requires rapid thinking and action. Cut yourself off from negative ideas as soon as you notice you are having them. "STOP" should be yelled either inside or outside. Don't pay attention to the bad thoughts, don't dispute with them, don't defend yourself, don't analyze them. Simply chop it off as though it were non-existent. Think about something else right now, or get up and do something else right away. Distract yourself from your negative thoughts by engaging in some kind of recreational activity.

2. Make a list of your ideas.

If chopping them off doesn't work, labeling them may be a better option. For the time being, recognize that what you are thinking is negative, but remind yourself that it is merely a thought. Whether you pay attention to it or ignore it, you are under no obligation to act on it since it is merely a thought and does not determine your actions. Negative ideas will only have an impact on you if you give them the authority to determine your behavior. Instead of focusing on how we question our ideas, we should consider how we respond to them. When we do nothing about them, we regain control over the situation. Consequently, tell yourself, "This is merely a bad thought, and I am under no obligation to do something about it."

3. Make your ideas seem bigger than they are.

Exaggerating the initial concept is another effective method of gaining control over your negative thinking patterns. Consider the following scenario: you are attempting to learn something and are failing miserably. You've been working on it for hours and you're starting to believe, "There's no use in trying; I'm simply dumb and will never learn," you say to yourself. Recognize that this is a terrible situation, and then exaggerate it to the point of becoming ridiculous and amusing. So say something like, "Yes, in fact, I am so dumb that I couldn't even screw in a light bulb if I tried." Or something likes it. And since I am so oblivious, everyone will notice and laugh at my expense. Following their laughter, I will give them another cause to laugh by jumping about like a kangaroo and shouting like a donkey, to the point that everyone in the room, including myself, will break out laughing. After that, I'll demonstrate to myself exactly how ridiculously foolish I can be. "Continue in this manner, using your creativity and being as caustic as you are capable of being, and refrain from taking whatever you say personally. I'm willing to wager that when you've completed this; your thoughts will be calm.

4. Counteract

This approach is diametrically opposed to the previous strategy. The precise opposite of what your mind thinks when it says, "I'm so foolish," is what you should say. As a result, it would read, "I am the most intelligent person in this room." If your mind tells you, "I'll never be good enough," tell it, "I'll always be good enough." It will work. When your mind tells you, "I'm too dumb to grasp this stuff," say, "I'm too clever to understand this stuff." This will counteract your mind's statement. This works because when we dwell on our negative ideas for too long, we are more likely to worry that we will act on those thoughts. And when we are afraid of acting on them, the fear almost always comes true because we wind up doing what we were trying so hard not to do because we were paying too much attention to it in the first place. When we speak the opposite of our ideas, we aren't actually paying attention to them; rather, we are coercing our brains to think in a more positive manner.

5. Make it a point to use positive affirmations.

Create two positive affirmations for every negative idea that comes to mind. When your mind tells you that you aren't good enough, you might say, "I am glad to be enough for the world today." You can also add, "It's a good thing I am attractive, because if I allowed this negative thinking to get the better of me, I could truly ruin my life." To ensure that we are more focused on positive thinking than on negative thinking, we come up with two positive affirmations for every bad idea. Throughout the course of the day, you may feel so good about yourself that you begin to credit yourself for creating this positive state of mind.

CONCLUSION

I Hope you found my book on how to eliminate mental chatter helpful. Positive thinking practices, such as overthinking and excessive worrying, have been carefully examined, and I guarantee that all of the material in this book is accurate. The strategies that you will learn and practice throughout this book have been discussed and described by a large number of specialists and have been tried and tested by a large number of individuals. Investing your time, energy, and spirit in them will provide positive results.

My expectations for you from this point forward in your life are that you will continue to practice good tactics and truly acquire the skills to avoid negative thinking and unnecessary concern. After you have completed reading, the only suggestion I can give you is to go back and underline your favorite passages or fold the corner of a page so that you may refer to it later when you are in need. Thus, if you find yourself slipping backwards after attempting to move ahead, you will be able to quickly return to the section of this book that was most helpful to you and correct the situation.

I wish you more success in the future and stay well!

REFERENCES

https://www.samhsa.gov/find-help/national-helpline

https://www.verywellmind.com/how-to-know-when-youre-overthinking-5077069

https://www.abc.net.au/news/2022-01-27/hi-vis-reflective-cattle-eartags-to-prevent-car-crashes/100779328

https://en.wikipedia.org/wiki/Cognitive_behavioral_therapy

https://www.healthline.com/health/cognitive-distortions

https://courses.lumenlearning.com/boundless-management/chapter/decision-making-process/

https://quizlet.com/433900662/global-health-exam-2-flash-cards/

Printed in Great Britain
by Amazon